for STRINGS

by HARVEY S. WHISTLER and HERMAN A. HUMMEL

CONTENTS

Units		PAGE NUMBERS		
		Strings	Piano	Score
1-16	Key of C Major	2	2	4
17-32	Key of G Major	4	5	10
33-48	Key of D Major	6	8	16
49-64	Key of A Major	8	11	22
65-80	Key of F Major	10	14	28
81-96	Key of B♭ Major	12	17	34
97-112	Key of E♭ Major	14	20	40
113-120	Chromatic Scales	16	23	46

7777 W. BLUEMOUND RD. P.O. BOX 13819 MILWAUKEE, WI 53213

VOLUMES IN THIS SERIES

ELEMENTARY SCALES AND BOWINGS for Strings

Violin (First Position)	**String Bass** (First Position)
Viola (First Position)	**Piano Accompaniment**
Cello (First Position)	**Full Score**

INTERMEDIATE SCALES AND BOWINGS for Strings

Violin (First Position)	**String Bass** (Easy Positions)
Viola (First Position)	**Piano Accompaniment**
Cello (Easy Positions)	**Full Score**

This Chart Is Included on the Inside Front Cover of each String Part

ABBREVIATIONS and TERMINOLOGY

LH Lower half of bow **UH** Upper half of bow **WB** Whole bow
FR At frog (about six inches of bow) **M** At middle of bow **P** At point (about six inches of bow)

★ ☆ ★ ☆ ★ ☆ ★ ☆ ★ ☆ ★

Legato Smooth and connected; usually slurred.

Staccato Short and detached; each note may be played with a separate bow, or several or more notes may be played in the same bow.

Détaché Smooth, separate-stroke legato with all bow changes as imperceptible as possible.

Simile Continue in the same manner; in this publication the term refers to the style of bowing.

(0), (4), (2), etc. (Small numerals in parentheses, placed above or below notes) indicate alternate fingerings that may be employed.

⌐⎯ (Brackets over two notes) indicate half-steps. On the violin and viola the fingers should be close together, touching each other.

POSITION INDICATIONS

Ip., IIp., IIIp., etc. (Roman numerals) indicate the basic position to be used.

Cello and String Bass:

½p. = Half Position

Cello:

$+$ = Extended Position

$-$ = Lowered Position

PREFERRED FINGERING SYSTEM for FIRST POSITION SCALES
(Violin and Viola)

When ASCENDING the OPEN STRING is used unless it is: (1) preceded by a half-step, (2) the last note of a slur, (3) the last note of the scale, or (4) the last of a group of notes. In such cases, the FOURTH FINGER is used.

When DESCENDING the FOURTH FINGER is used unless it is: (1) preceded by a half-step, (2) the middle or last note of a slur, (3) the last note of a scale, or (4) the last of a group of notes. In such cases, the OPEN STRING is used.

Key of C Major

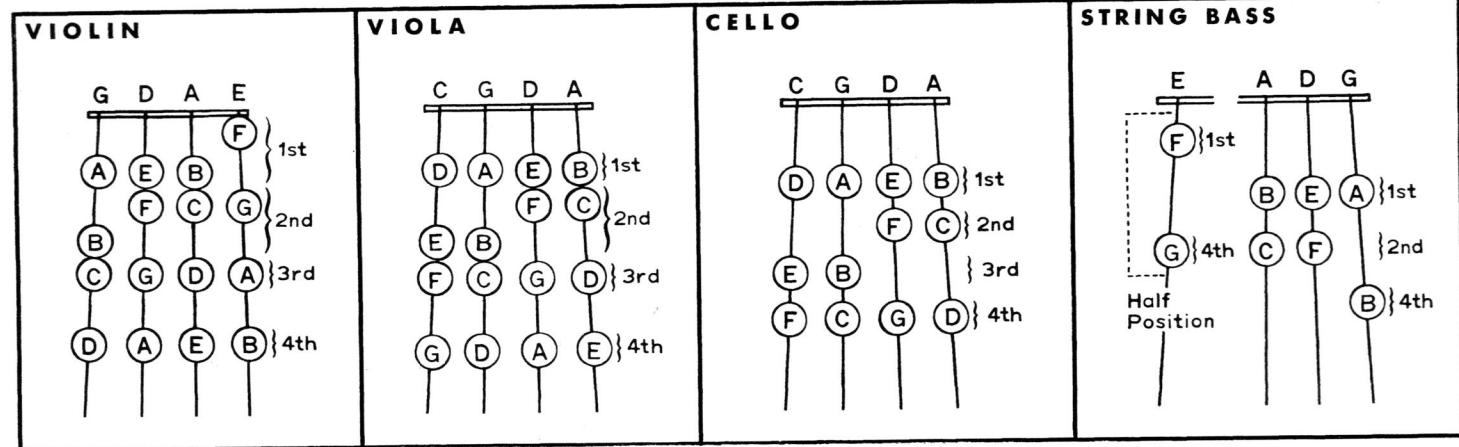

Détaché Scale

Slurred Scales

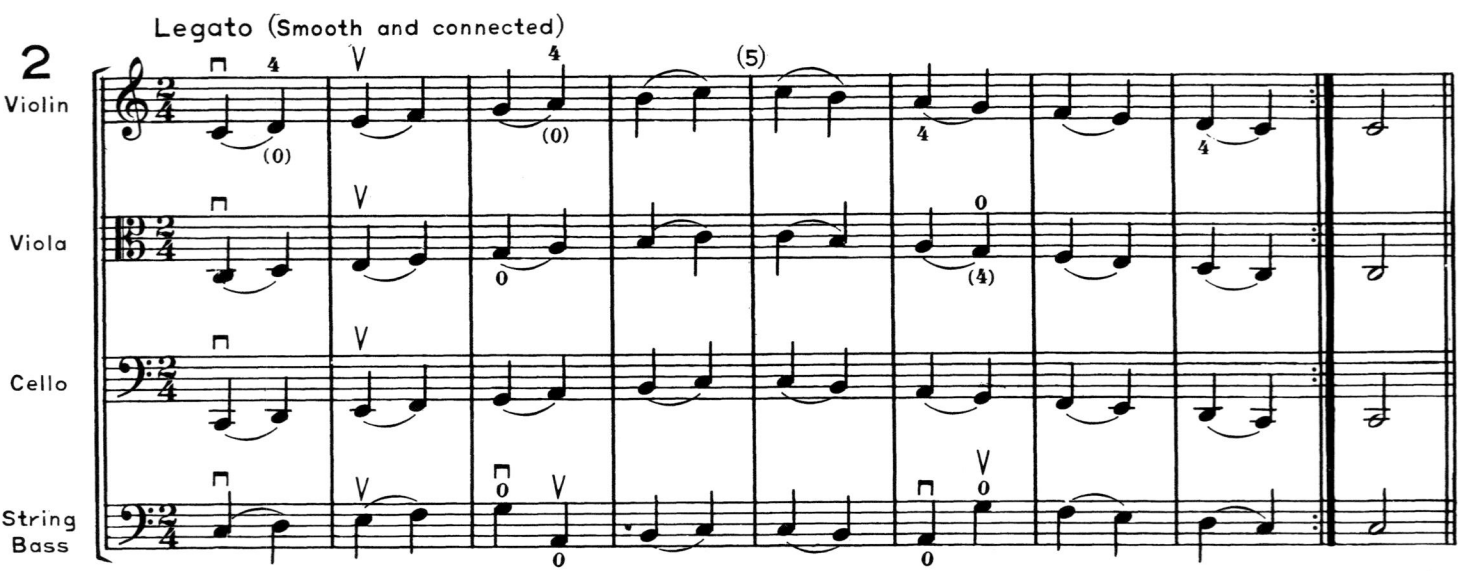

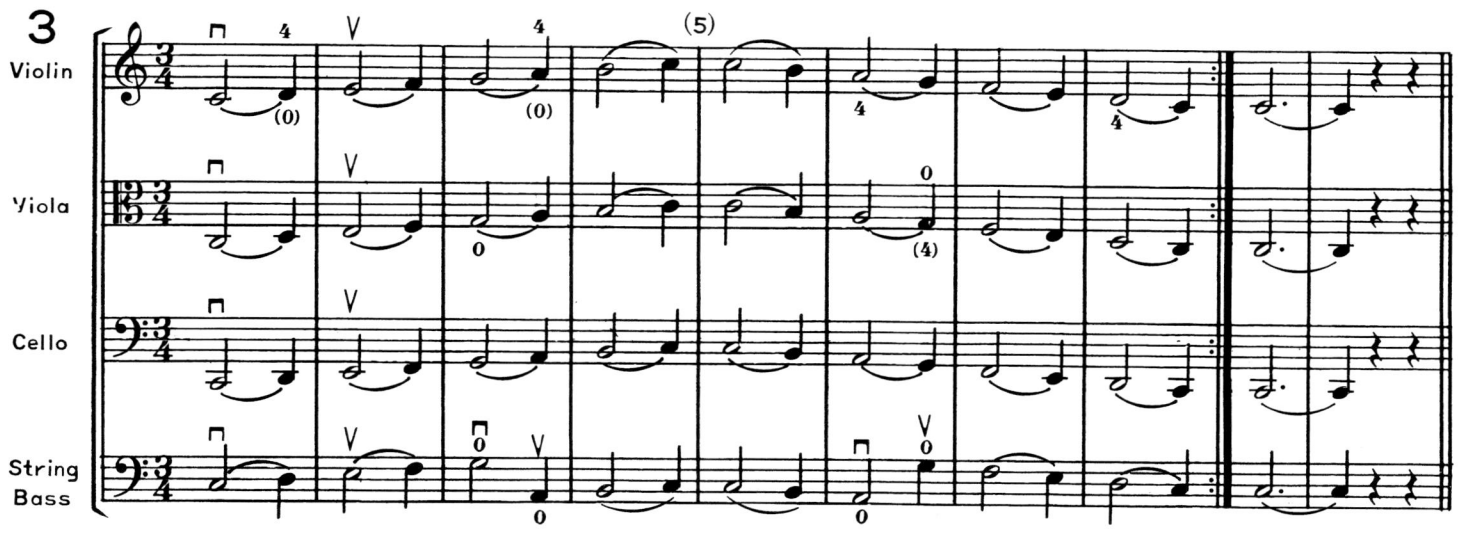

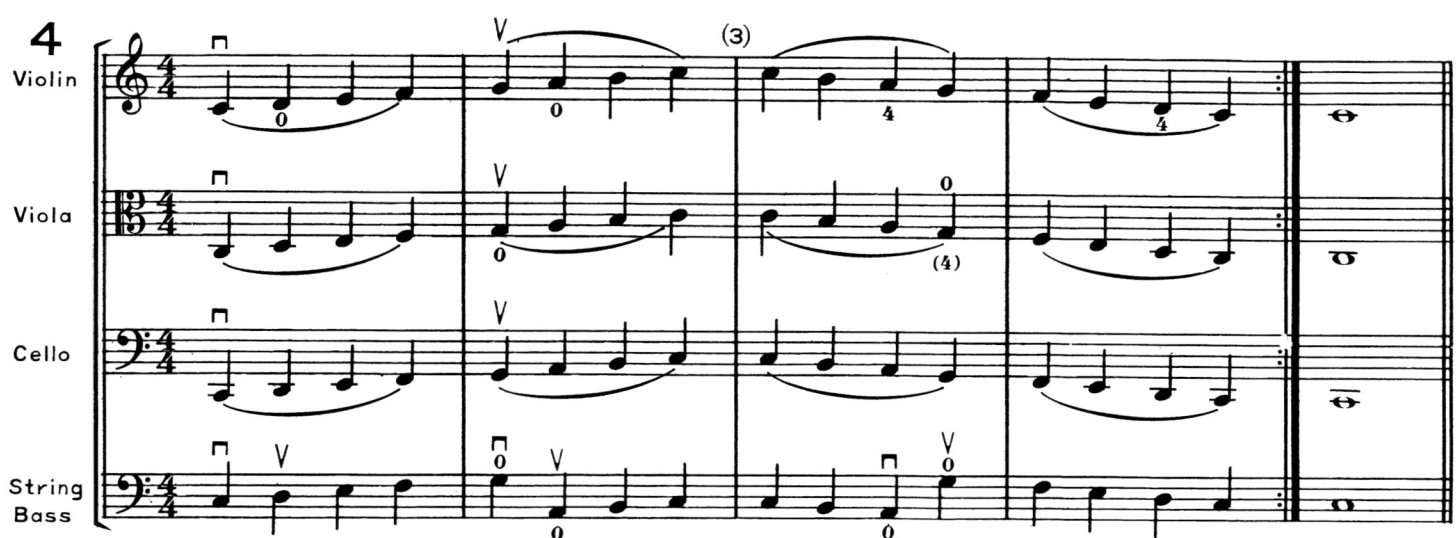

Detached Bowings

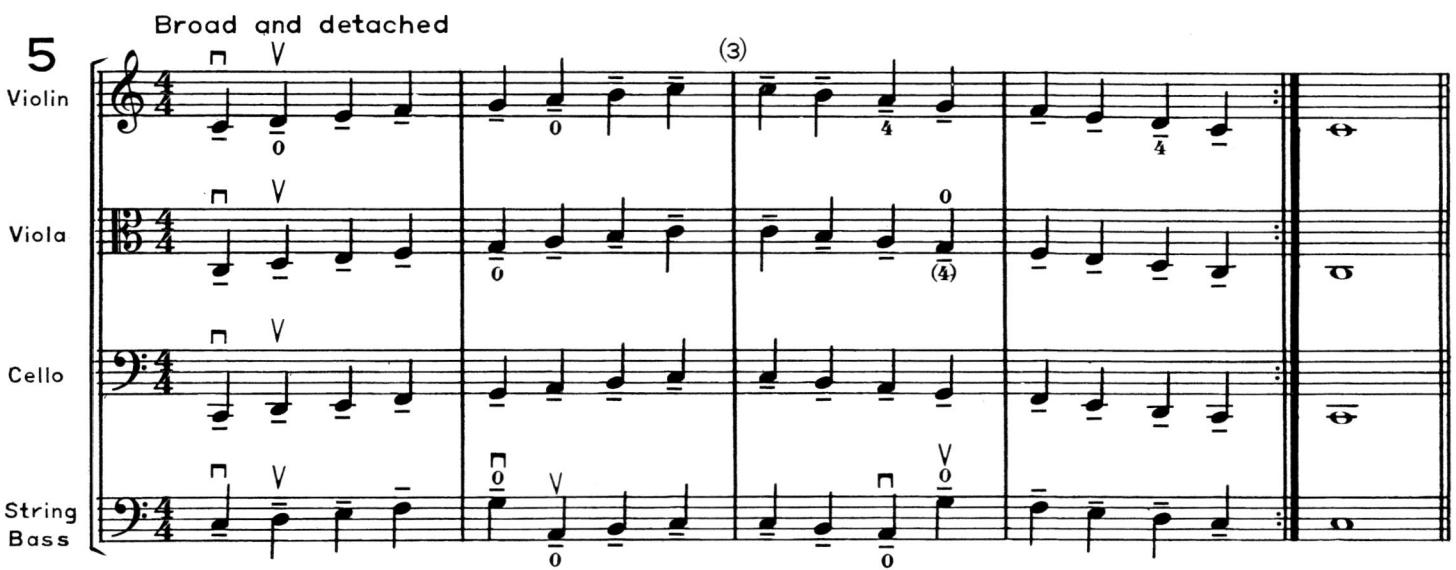

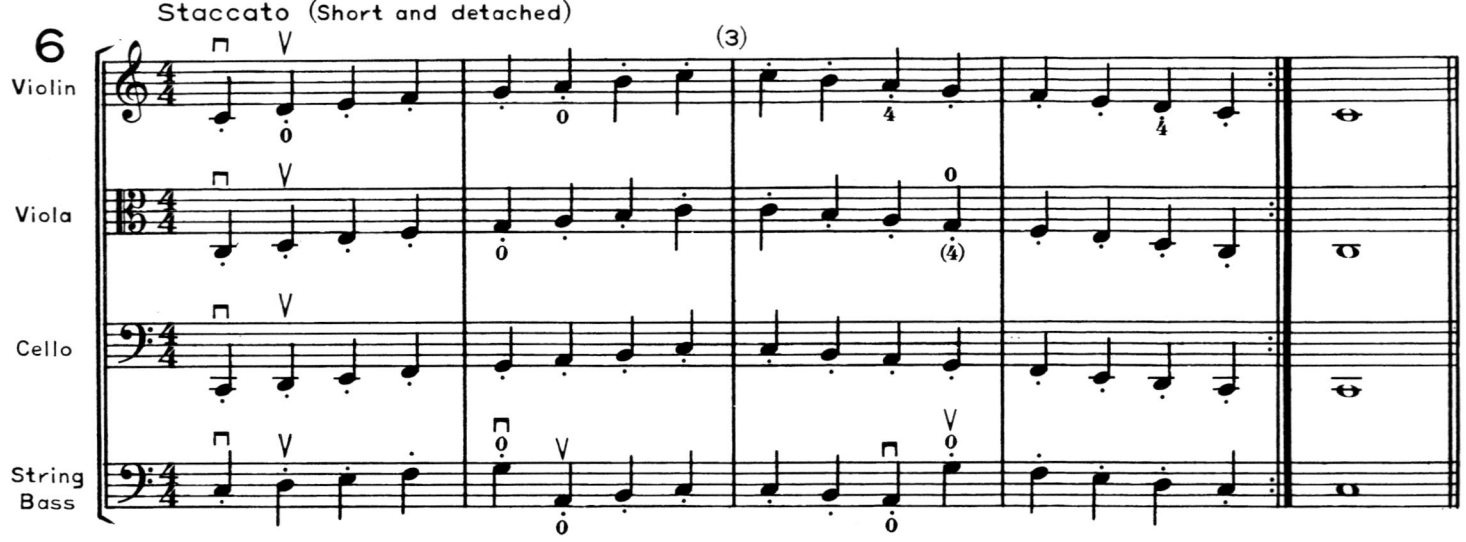

Bow Division

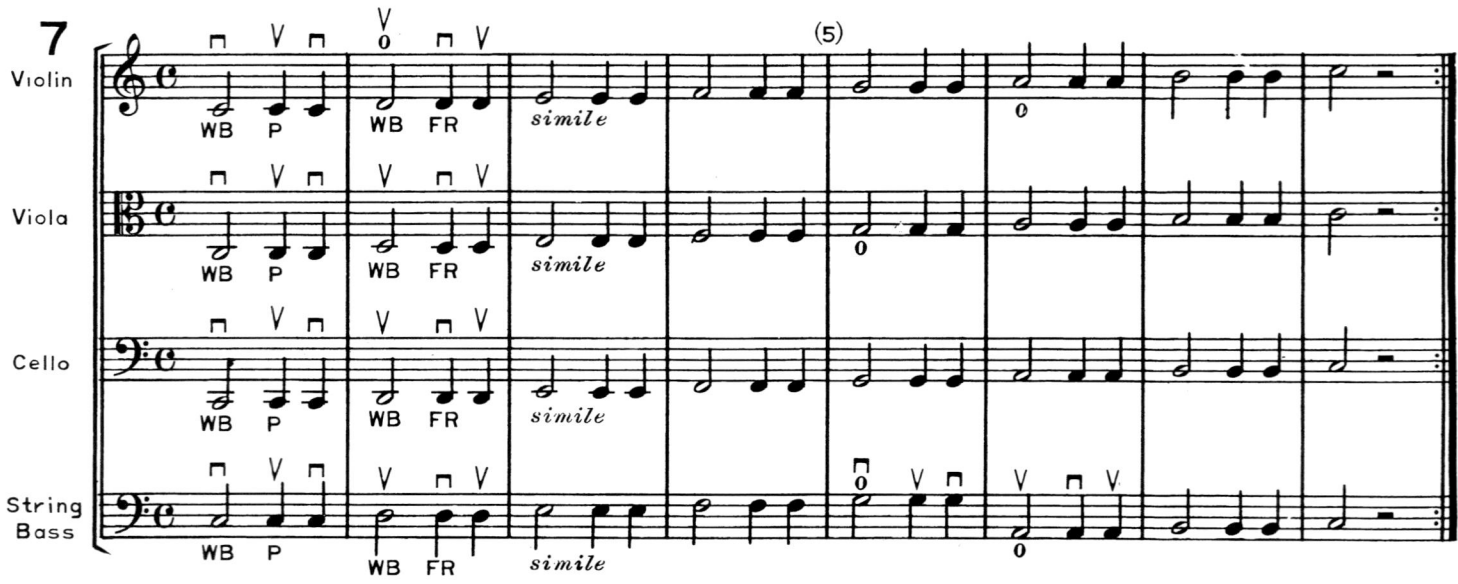

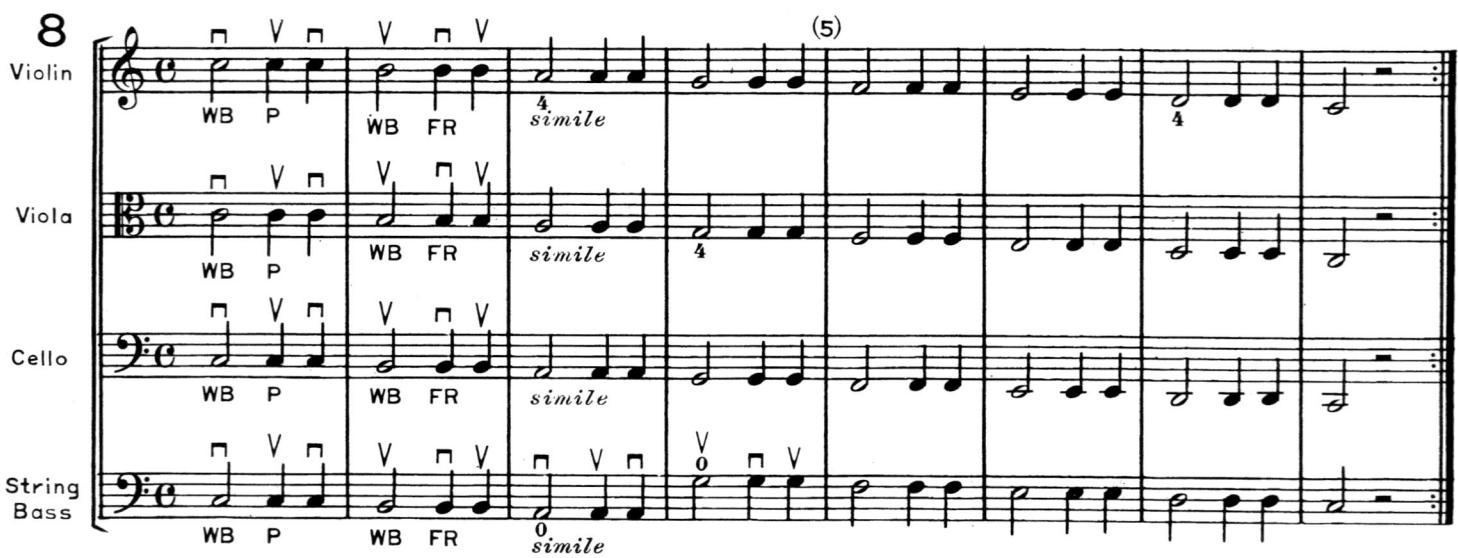

Détaché Scale in Quarter Notes

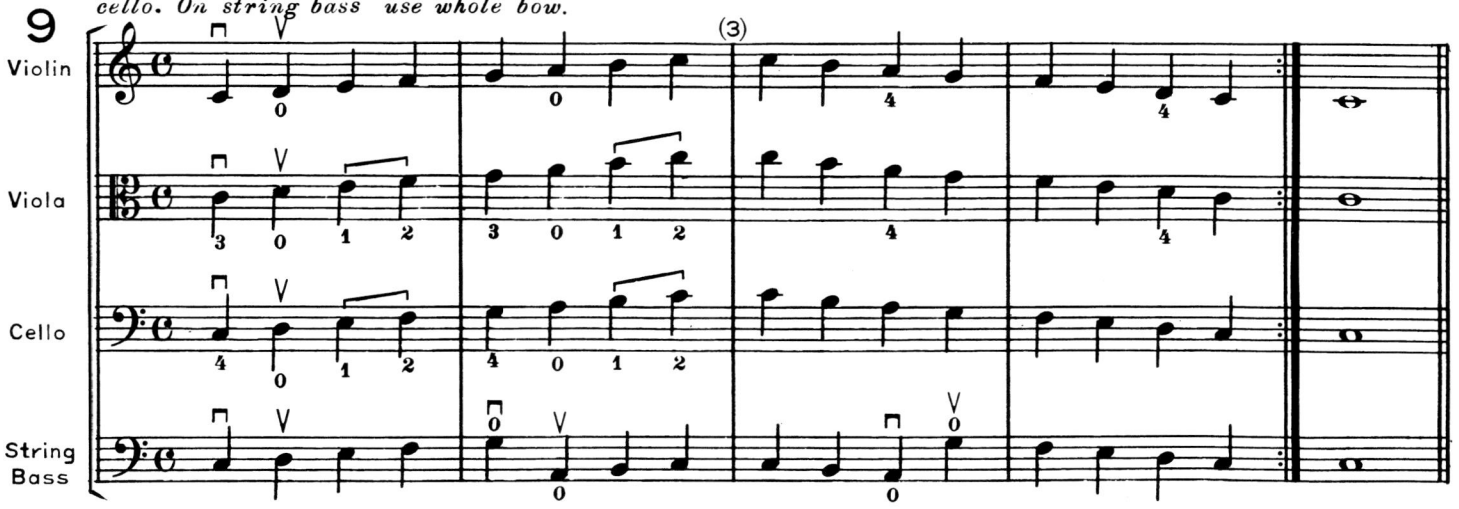

Broken Chords

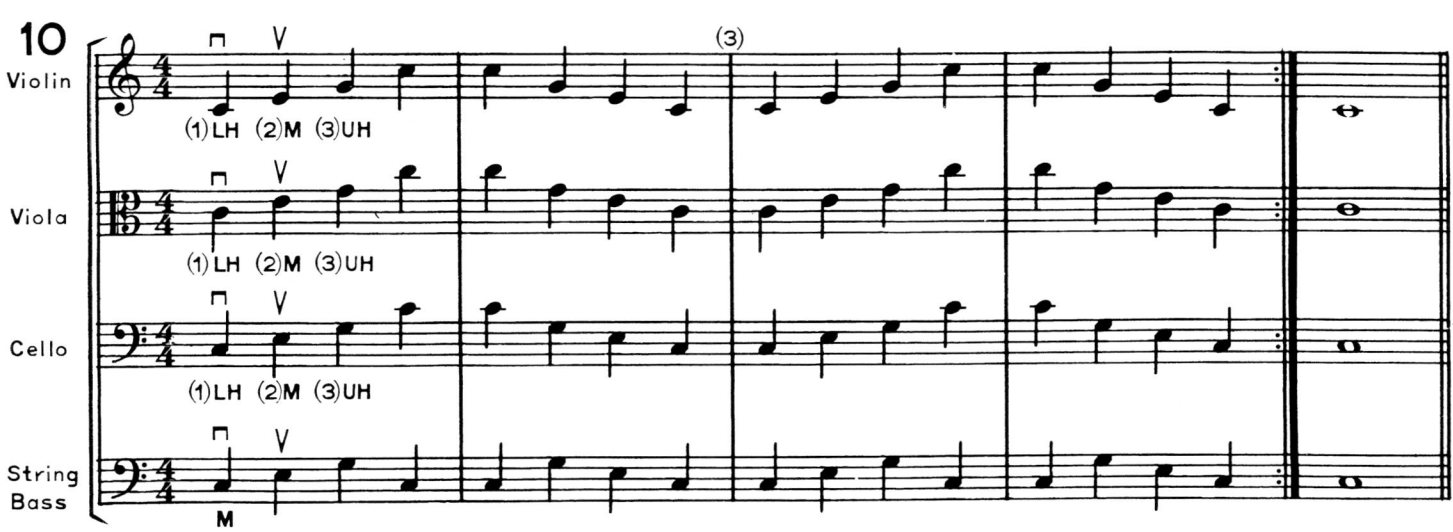

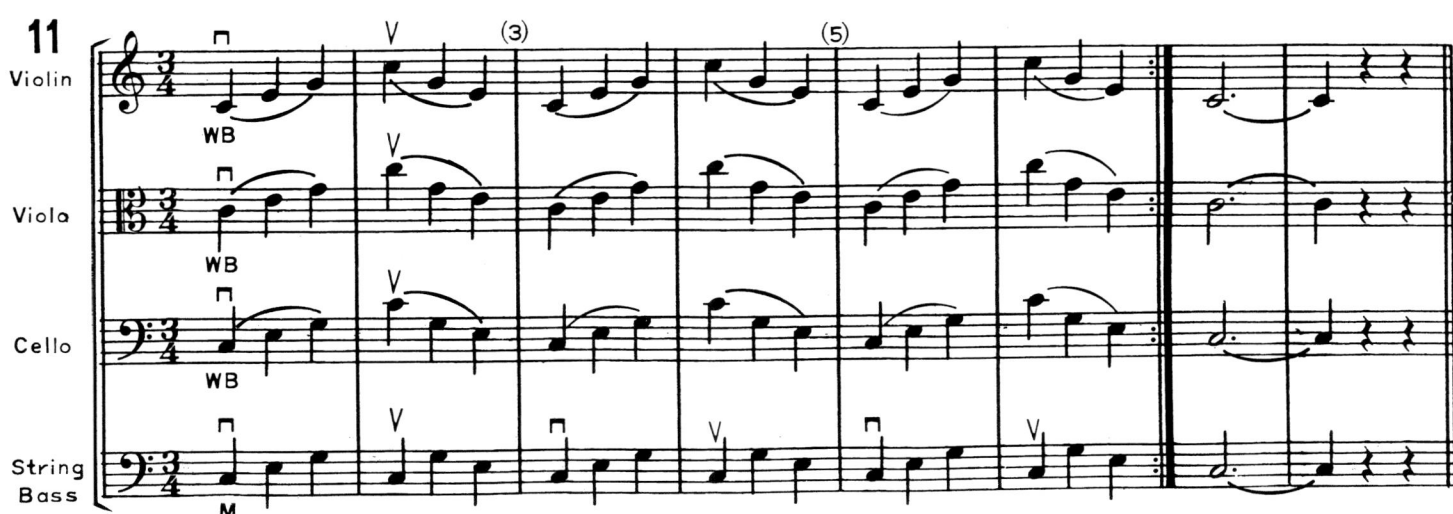

Tone Study

Eighth Notes

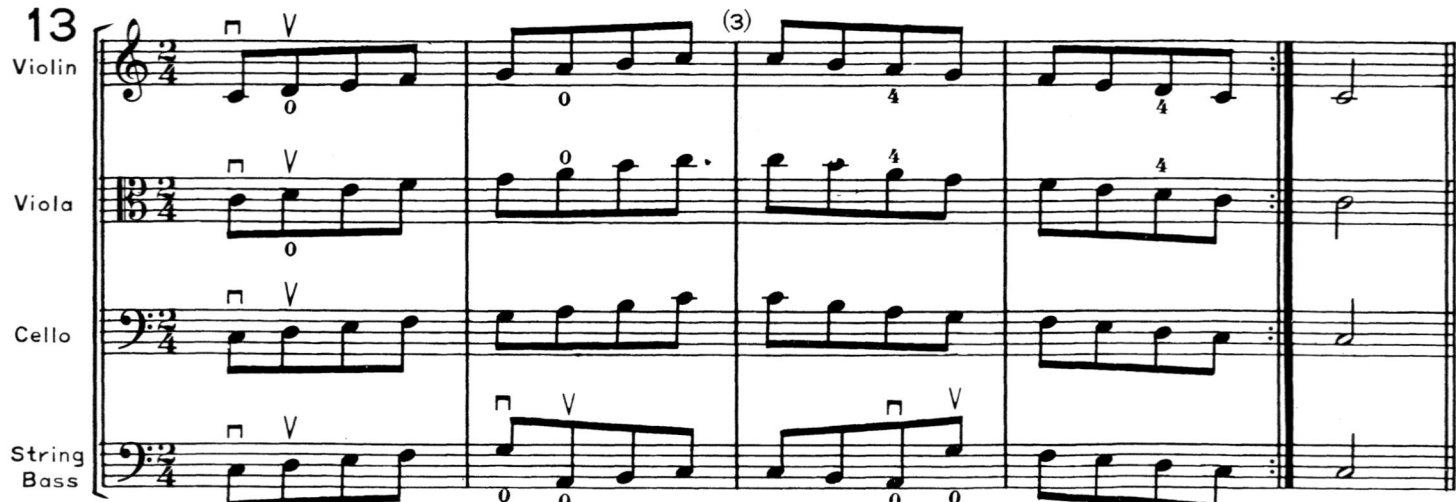

Quarter and Eighth Notes

Key of G Major

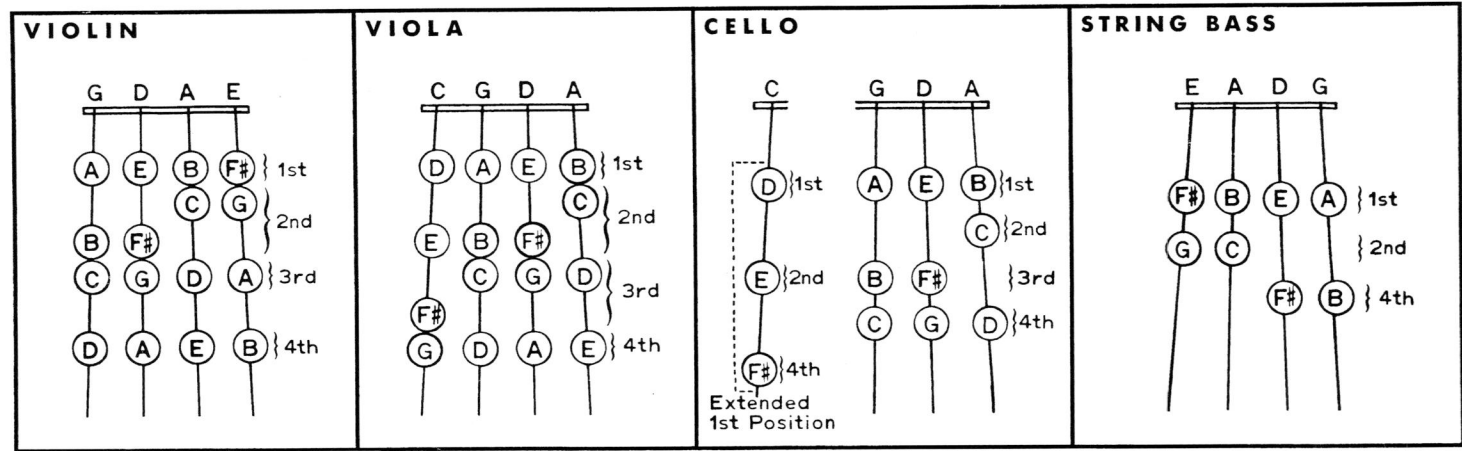

Détaché Scale

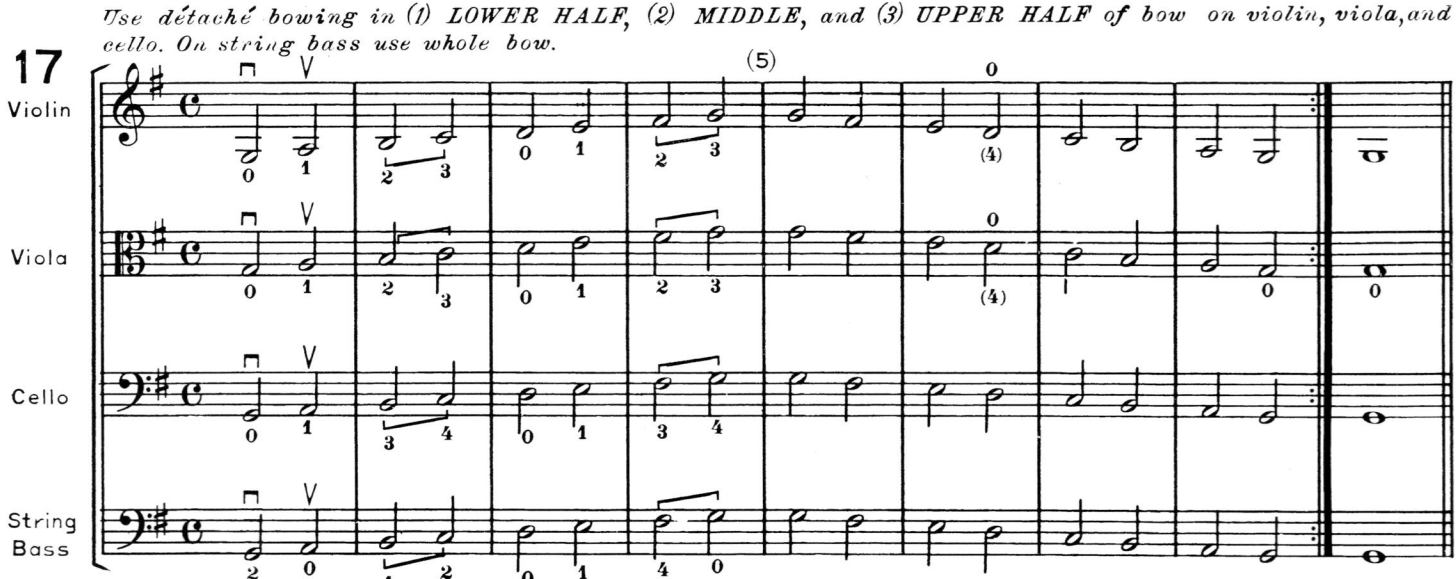

Slurred Scale

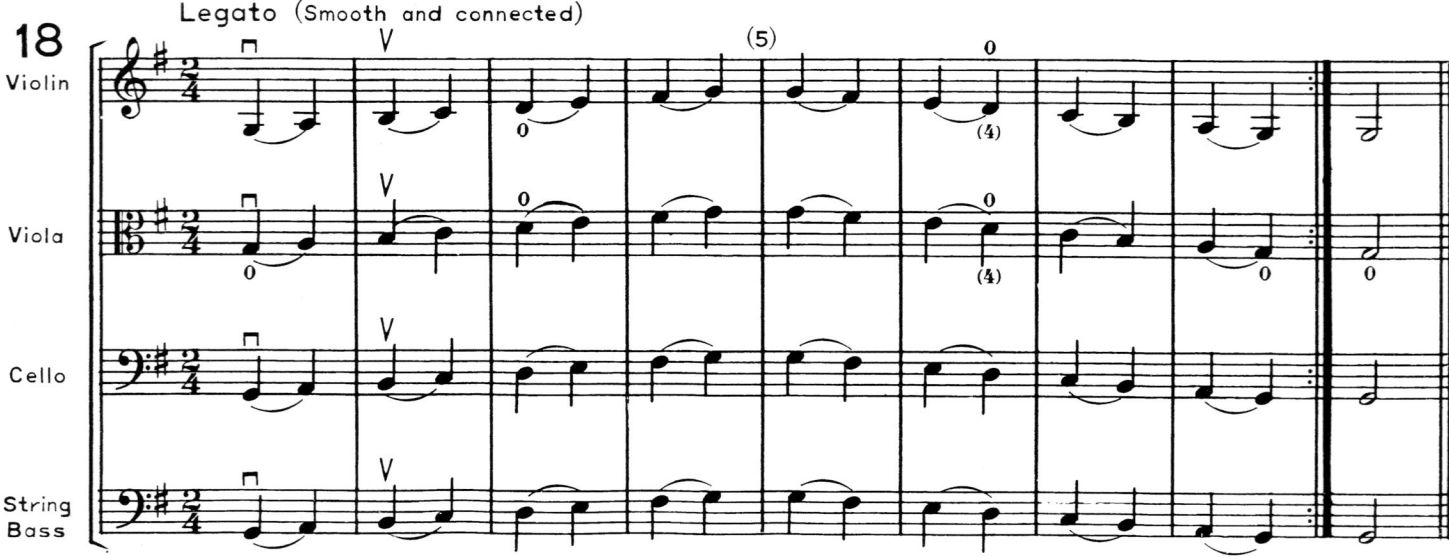

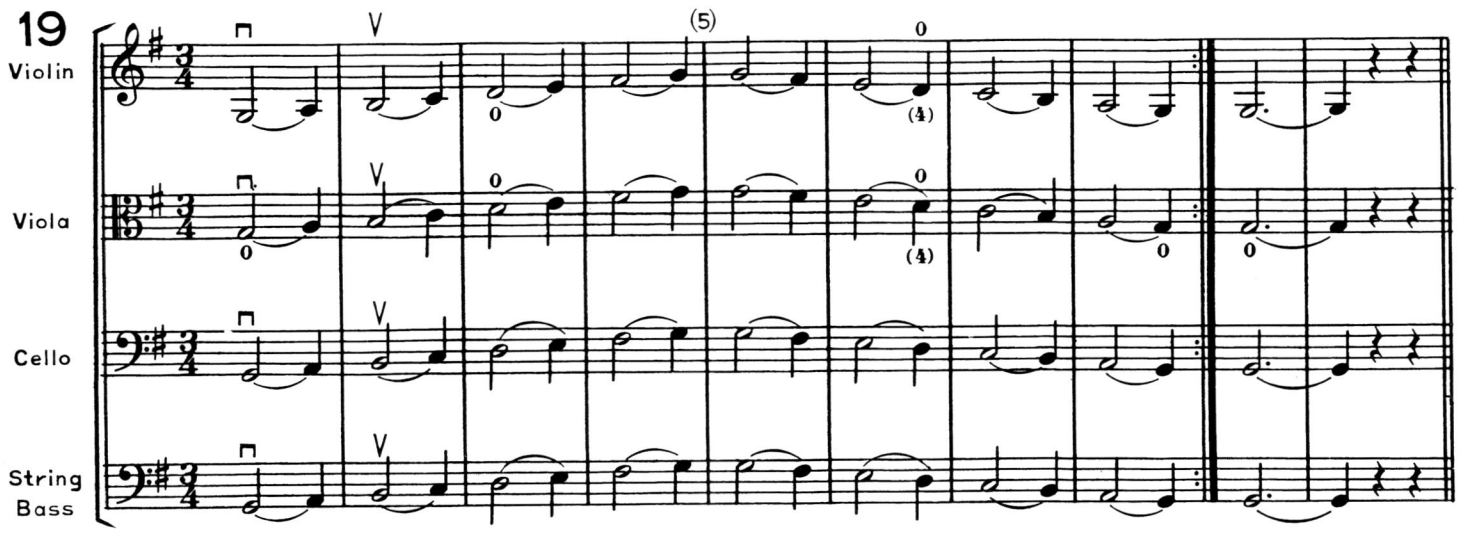

Detached Bowings

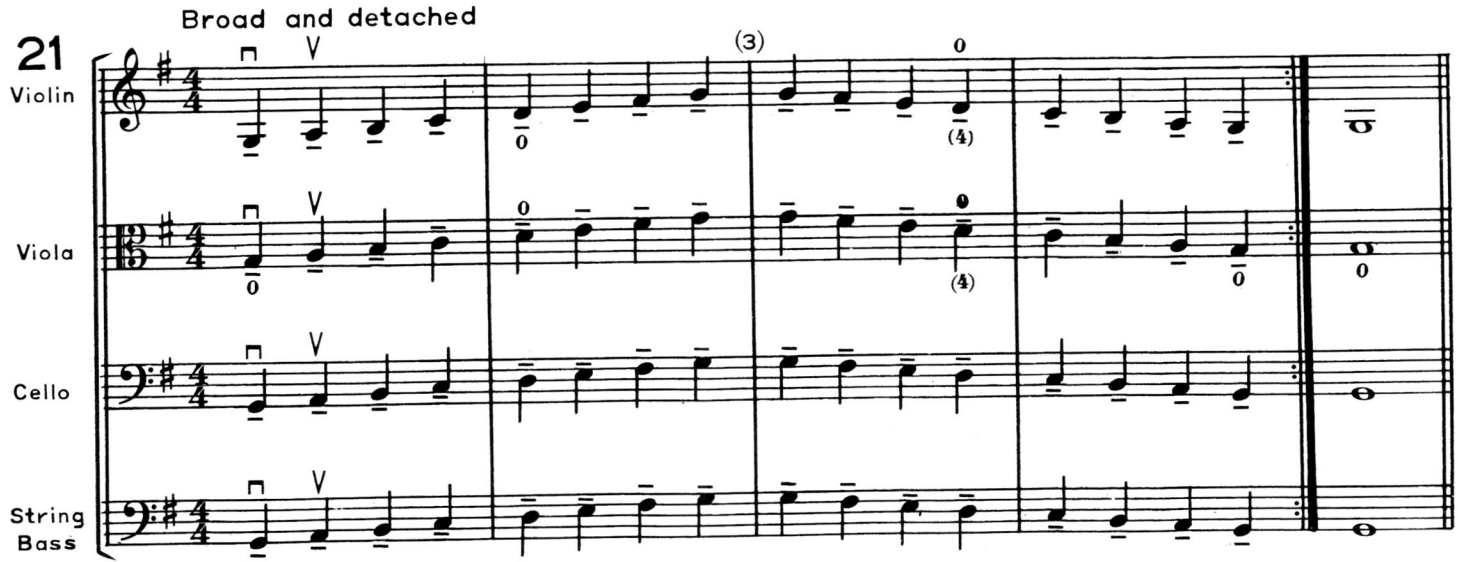

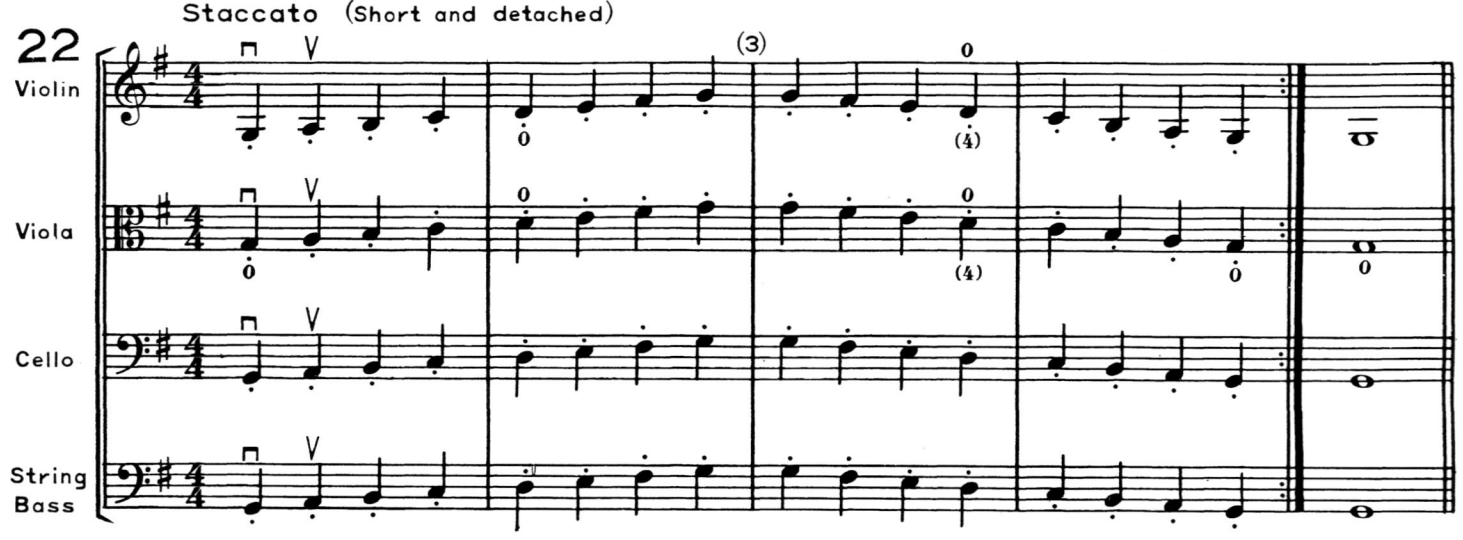

Bow Division

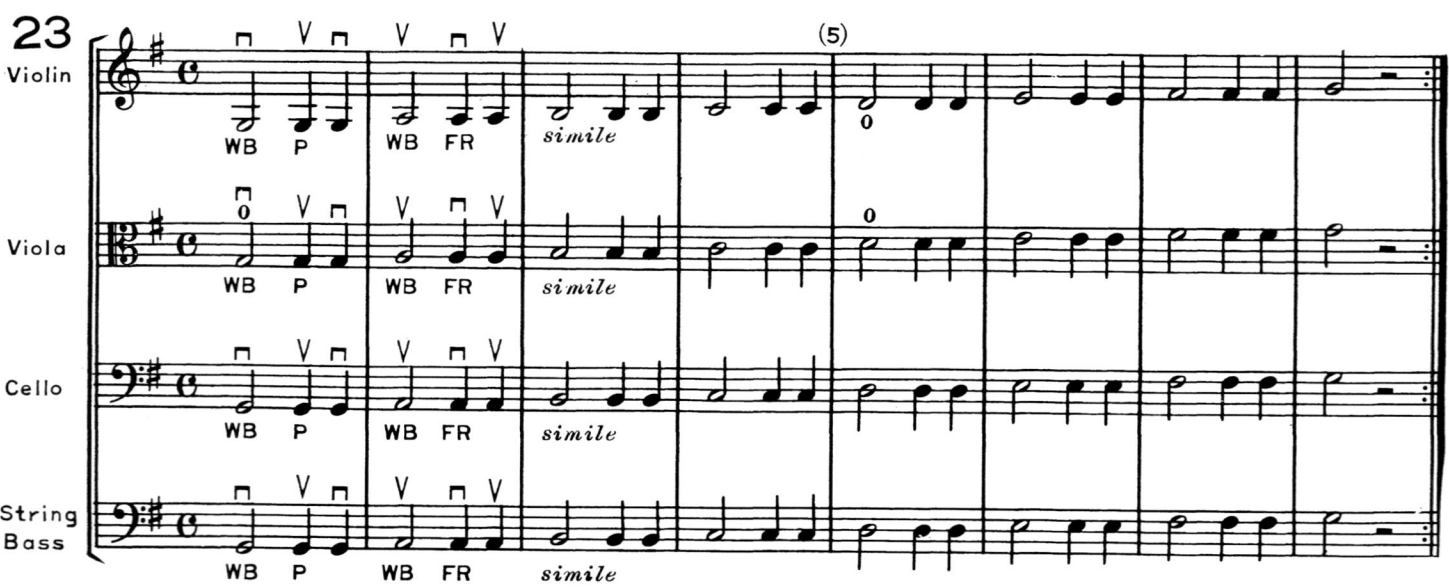

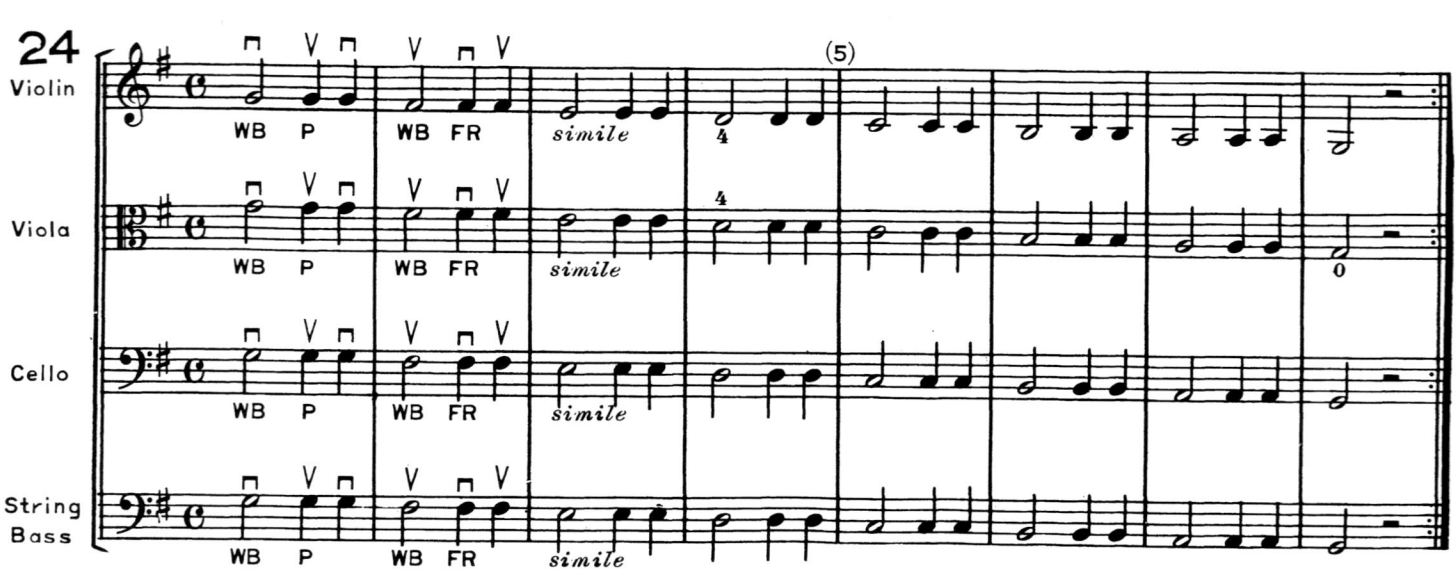

Détaché Scale in Quarter Notes

Use détaché bowing in (1) LOWER HALF, (2) MIDDLE, and (3) UPPER HALF of bow on violin, viola, and cello. On string bass use whole bow.

Broken Chords

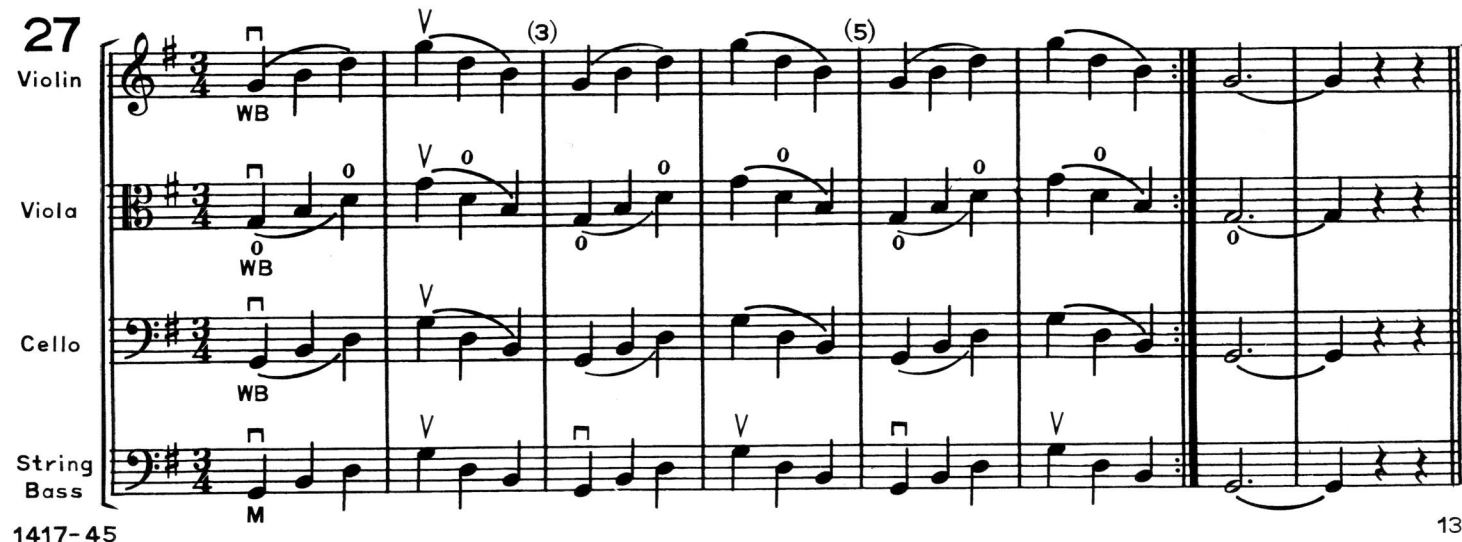

Tone Study

Also practice very slowly, sustaining each tone for EIGHT counts.

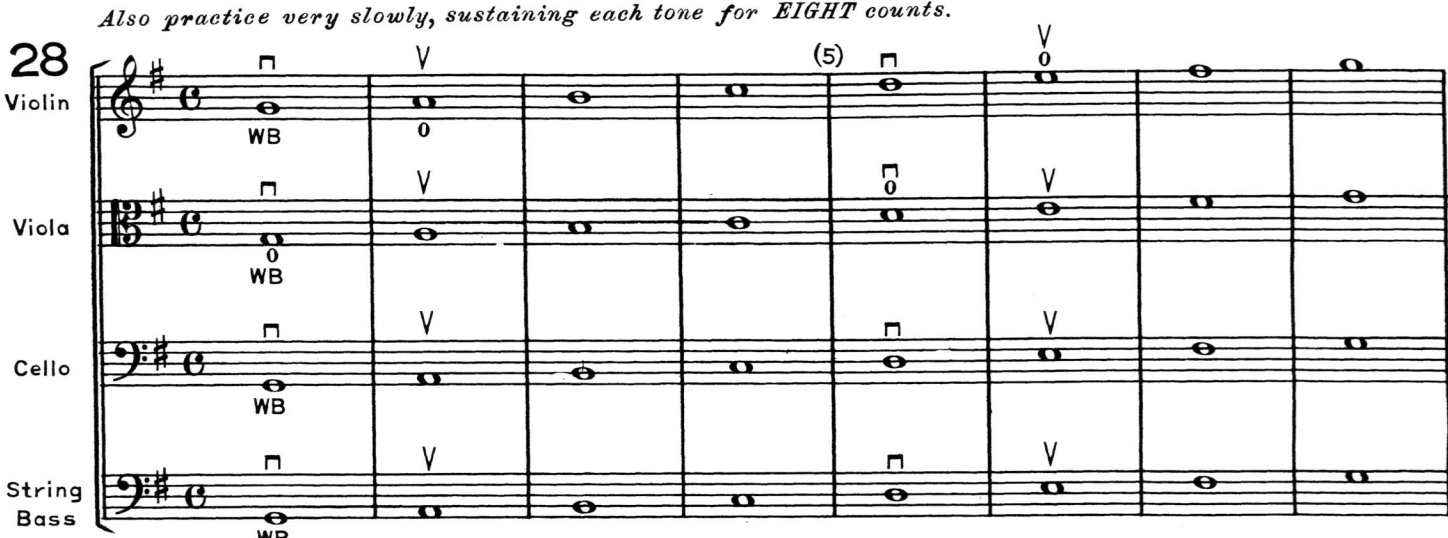

Eighth Notes

Also practice (1) slurring each TWO notes, and (2) slurring each FOUR notes.

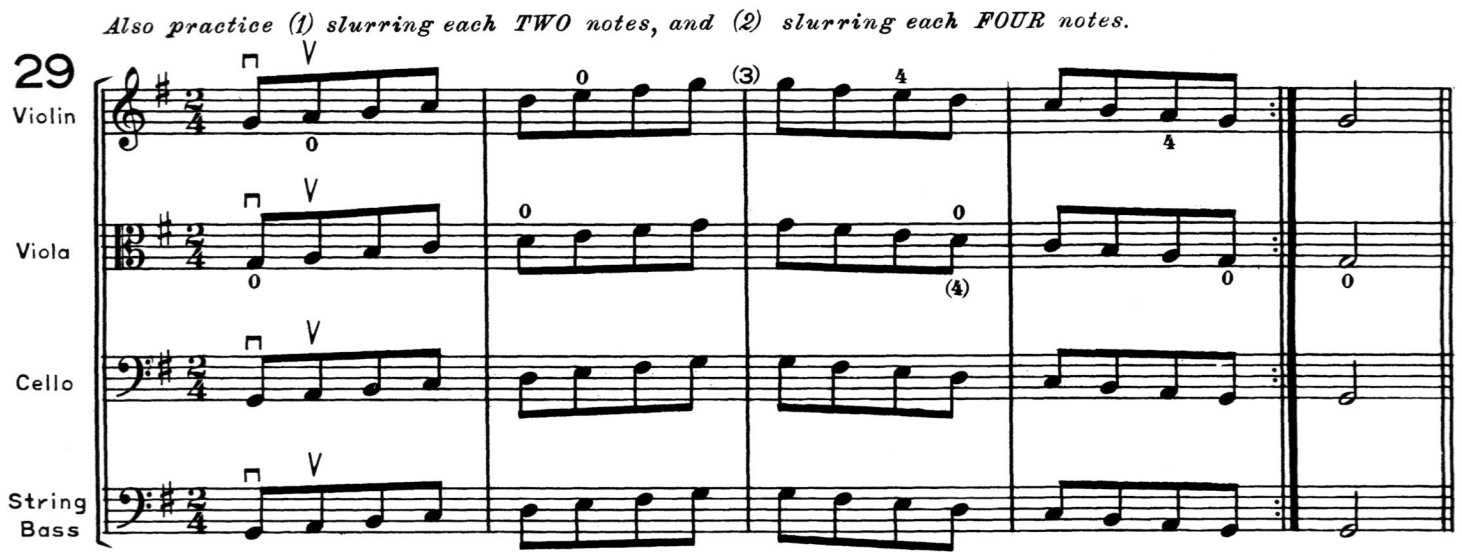

Quarter and Eighth Notes

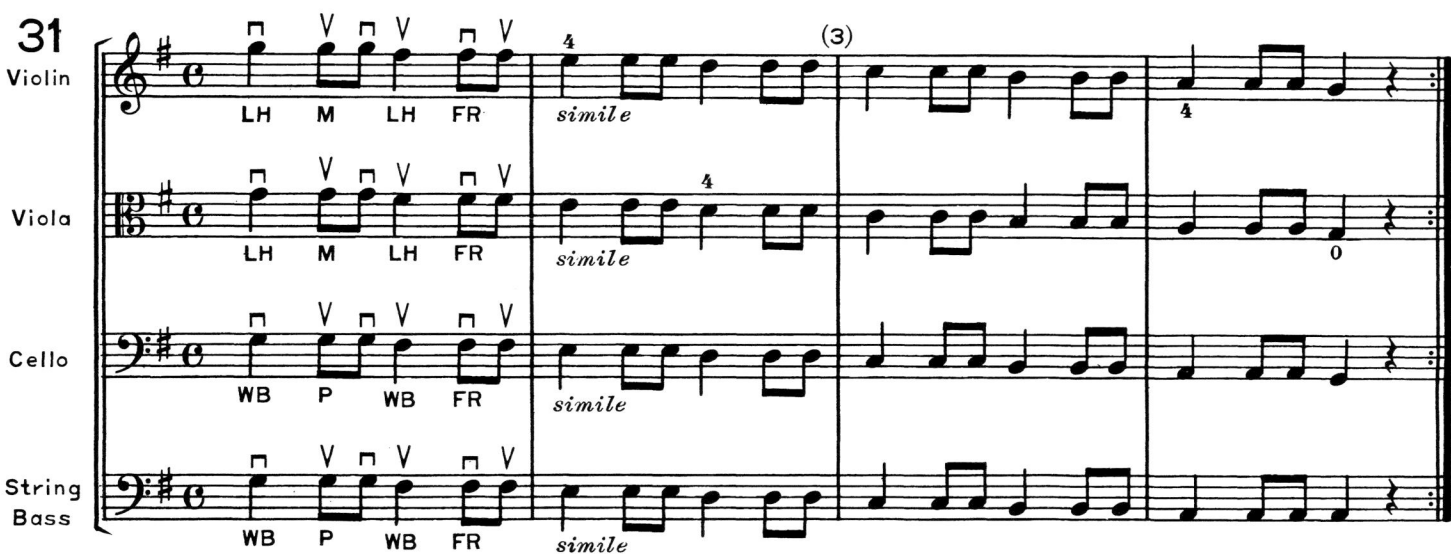

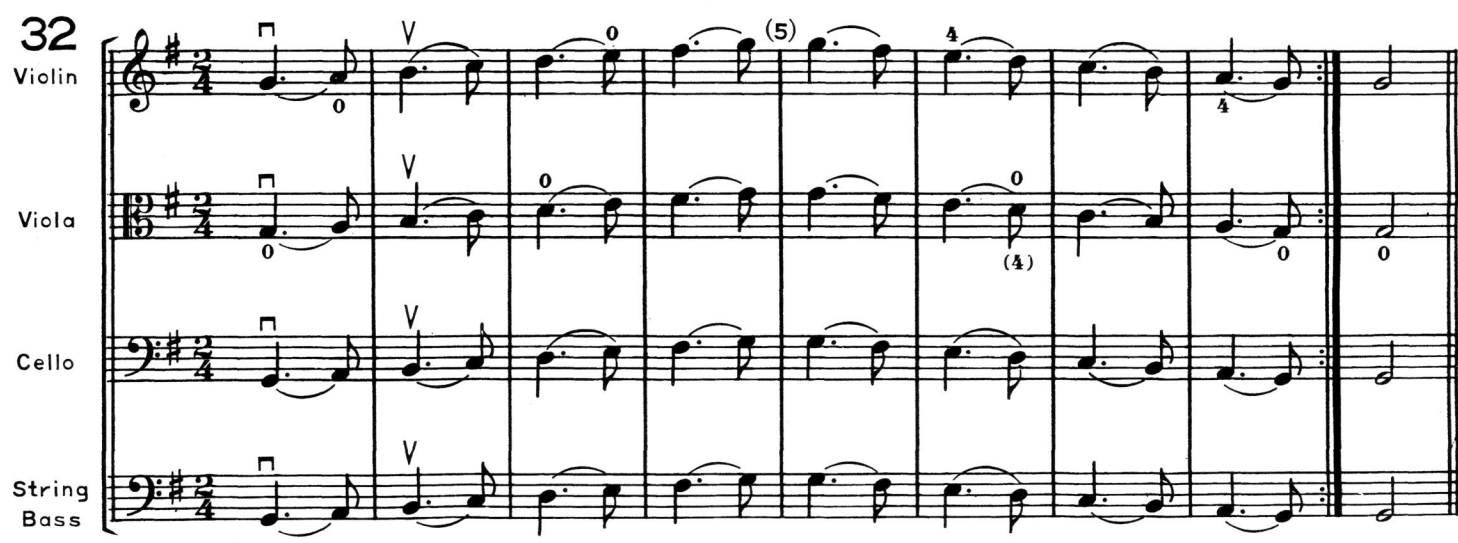

Key of D Major

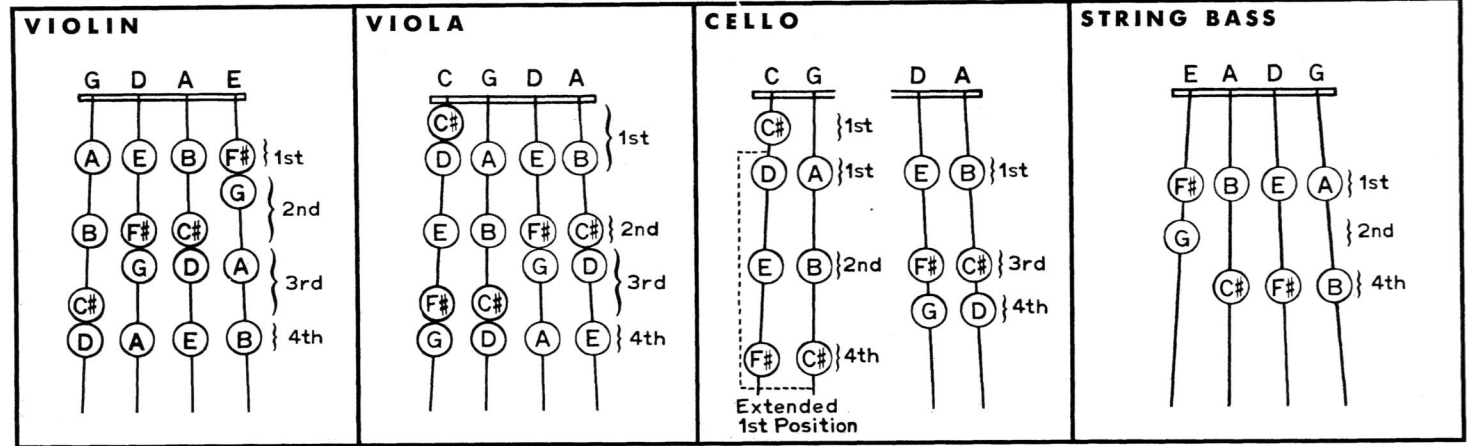

Détaché Scale

Slurred Scales

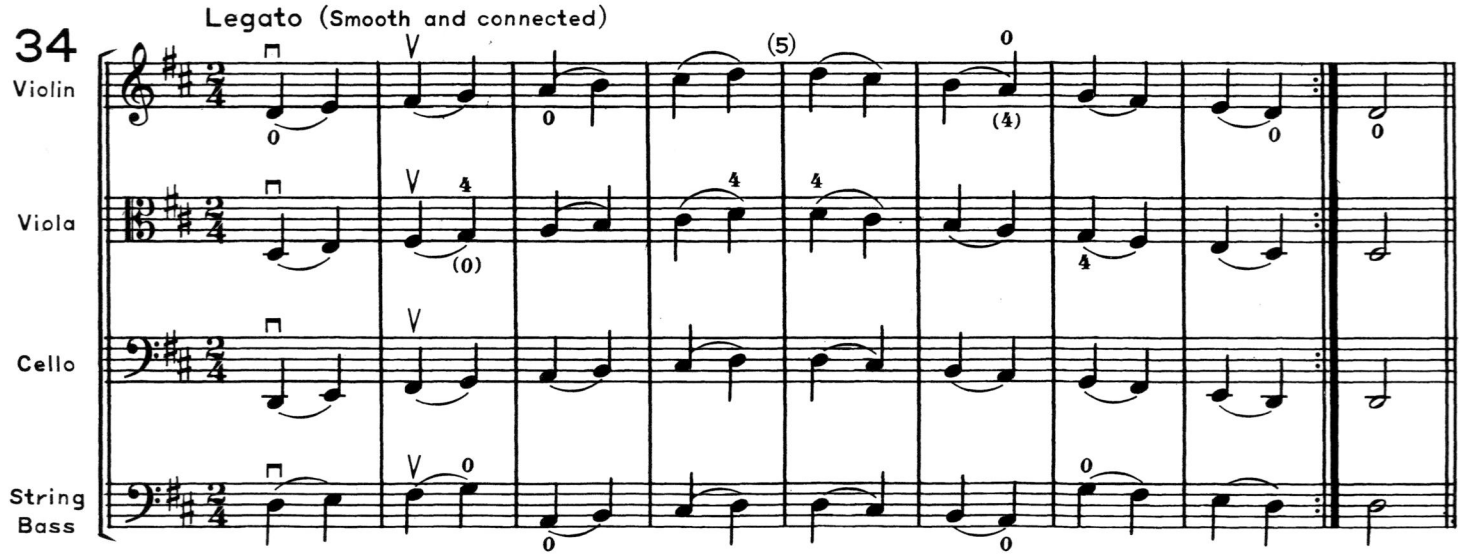

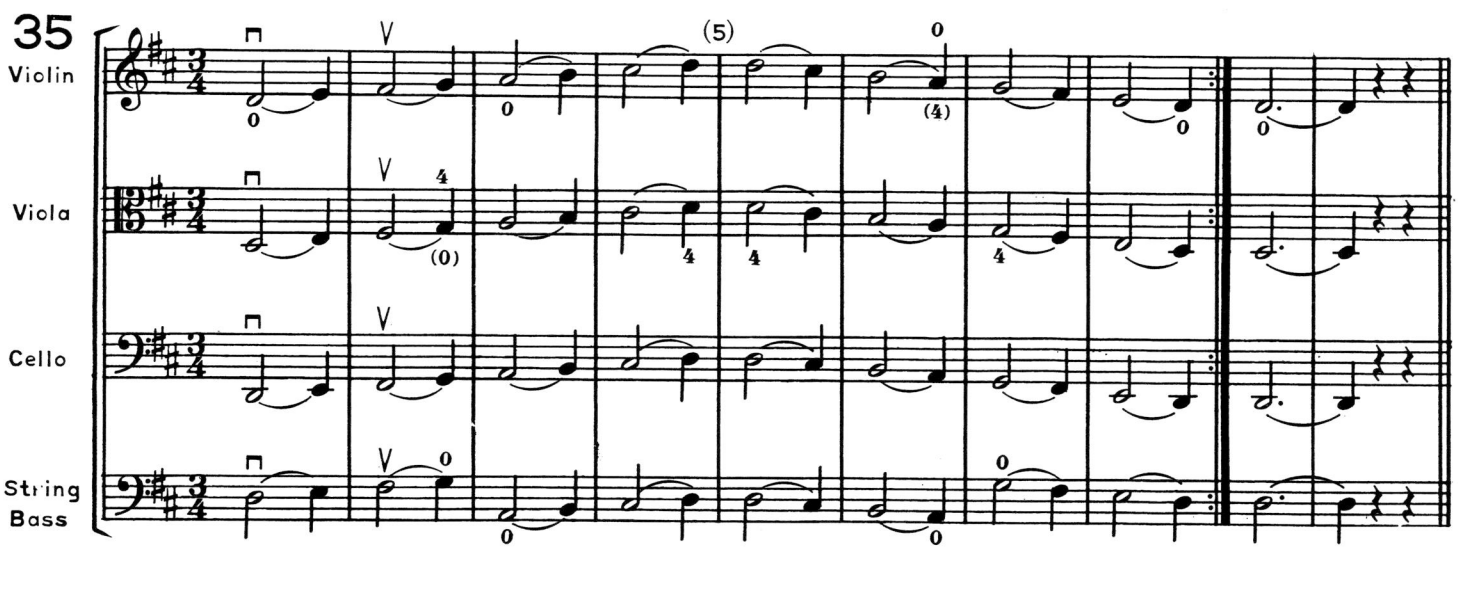

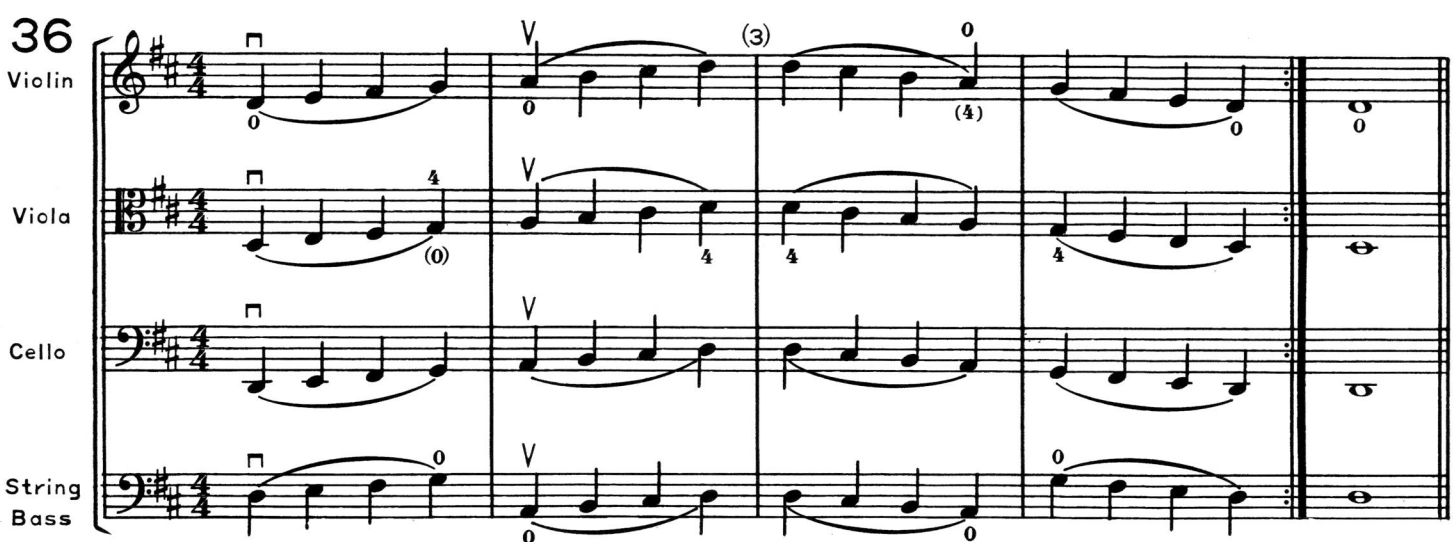

Detached Bowings

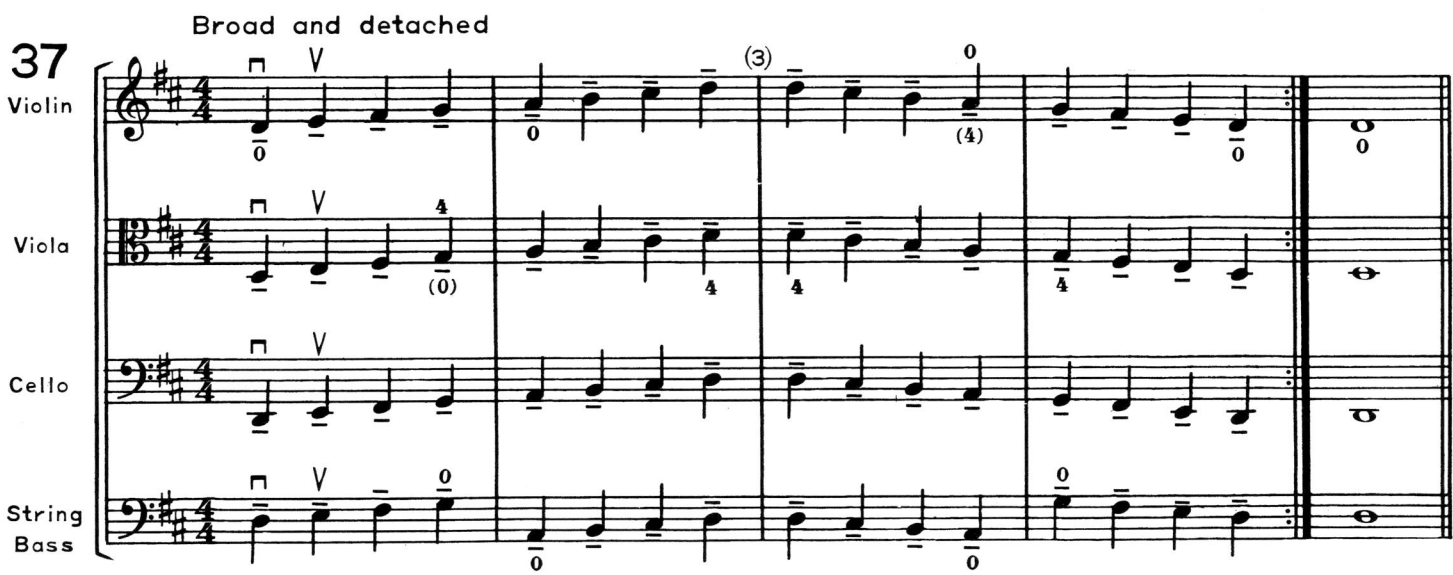

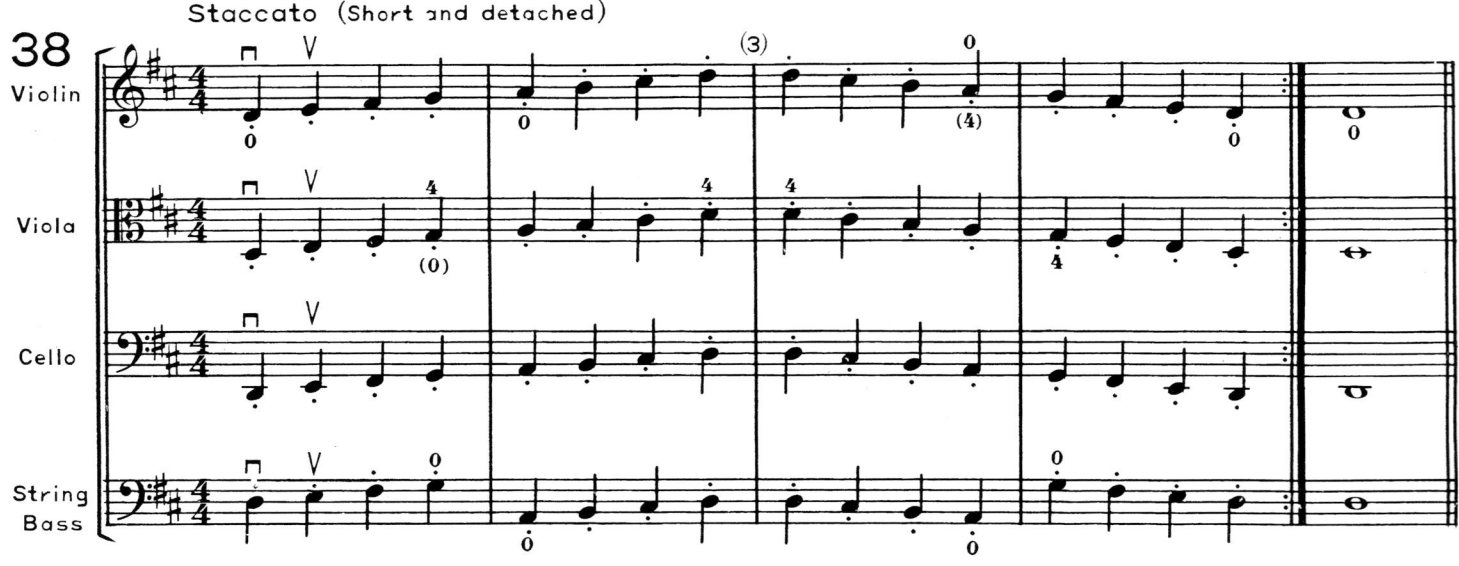

Bow Division

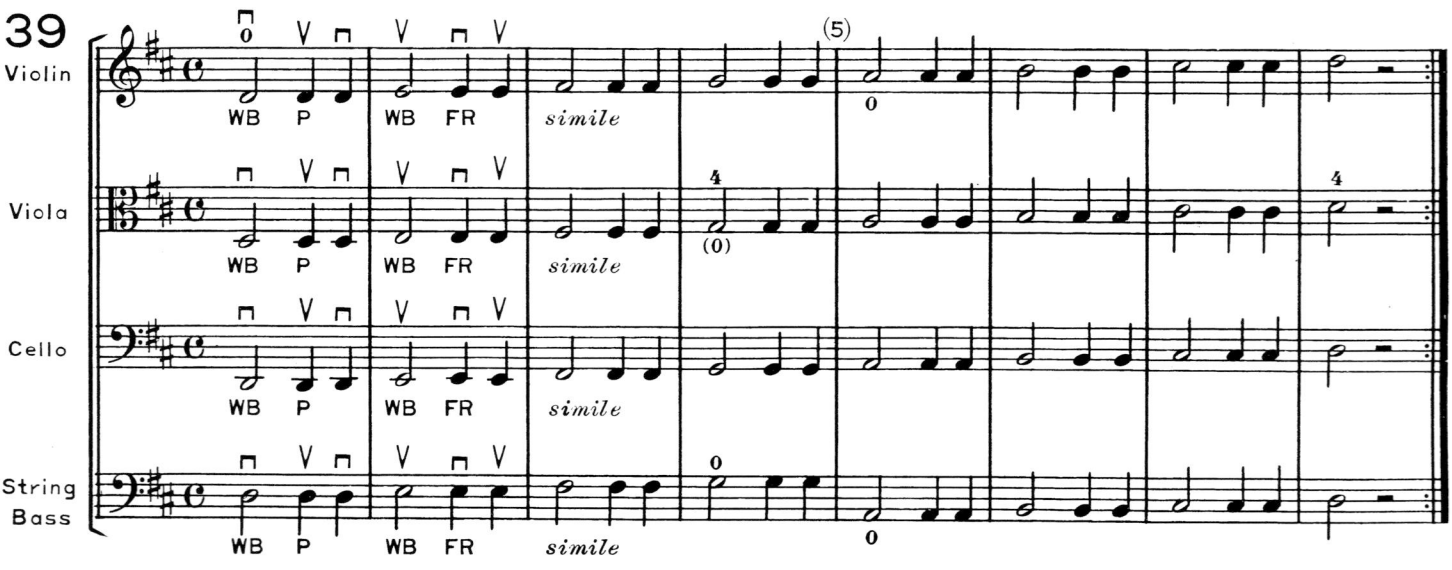

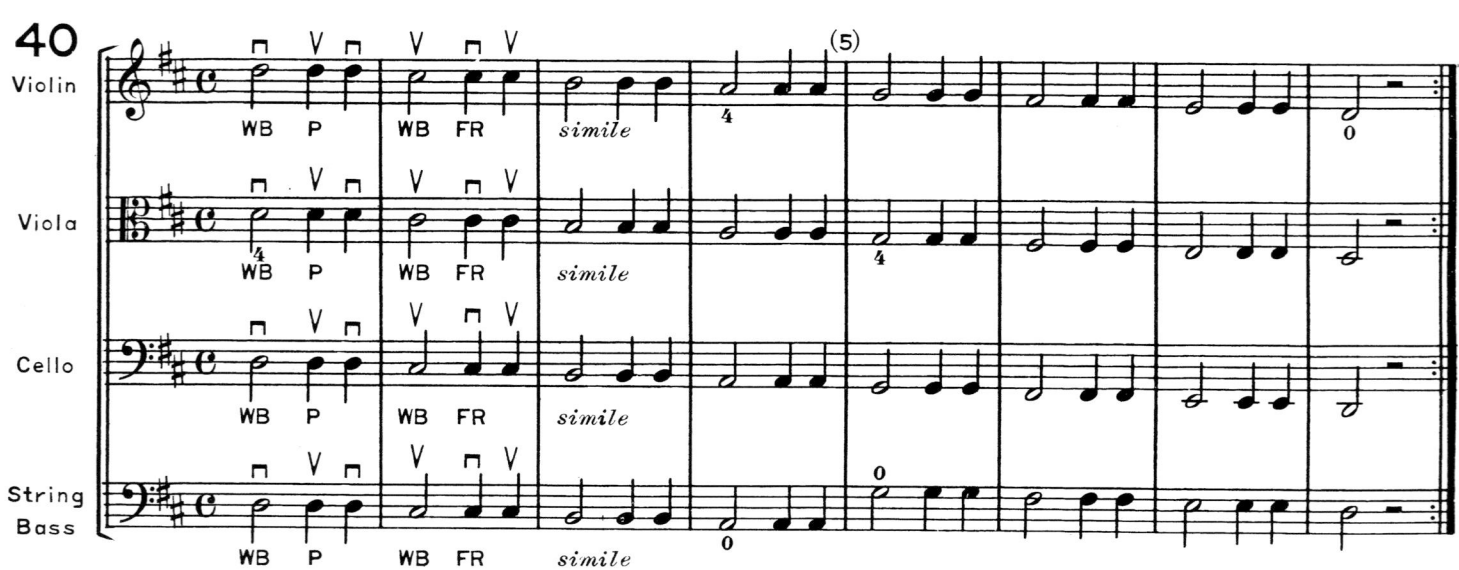

Détaché Scale in Quarter Notes

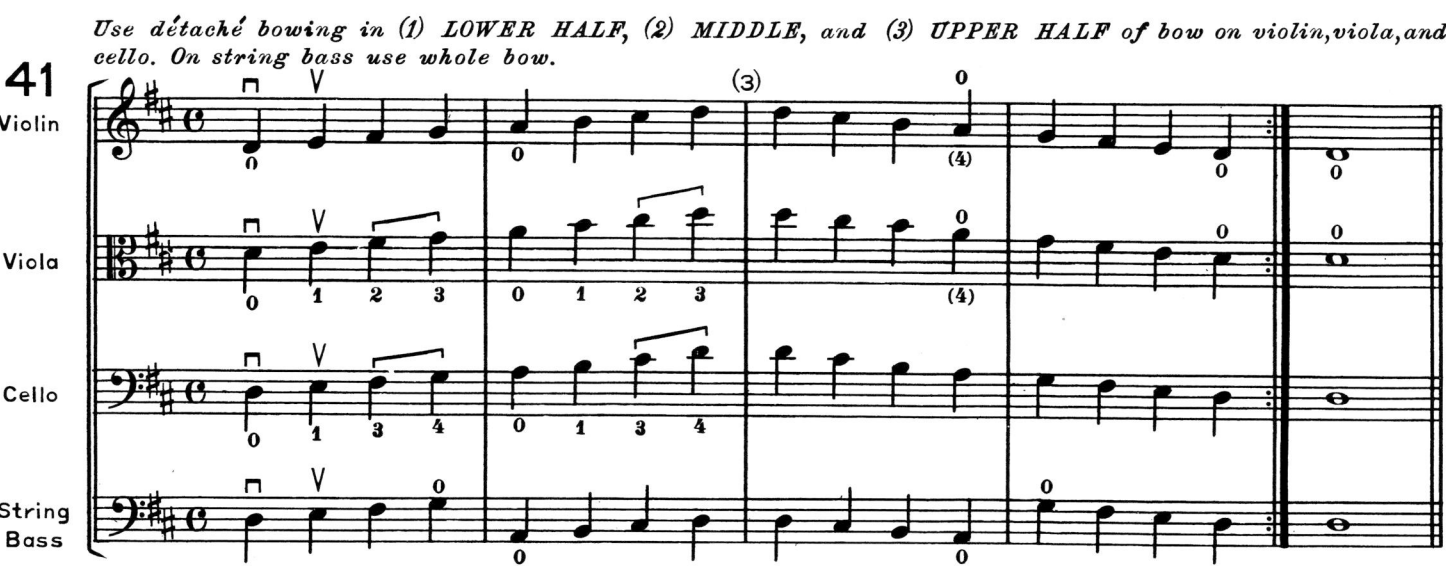

Use détaché bowing in (1) LOWER HALF, (2) MIDDLE, and (3) UPPER HALF of bow on violin, viola, and cello. On string bass use whole bow.

Broken Chords

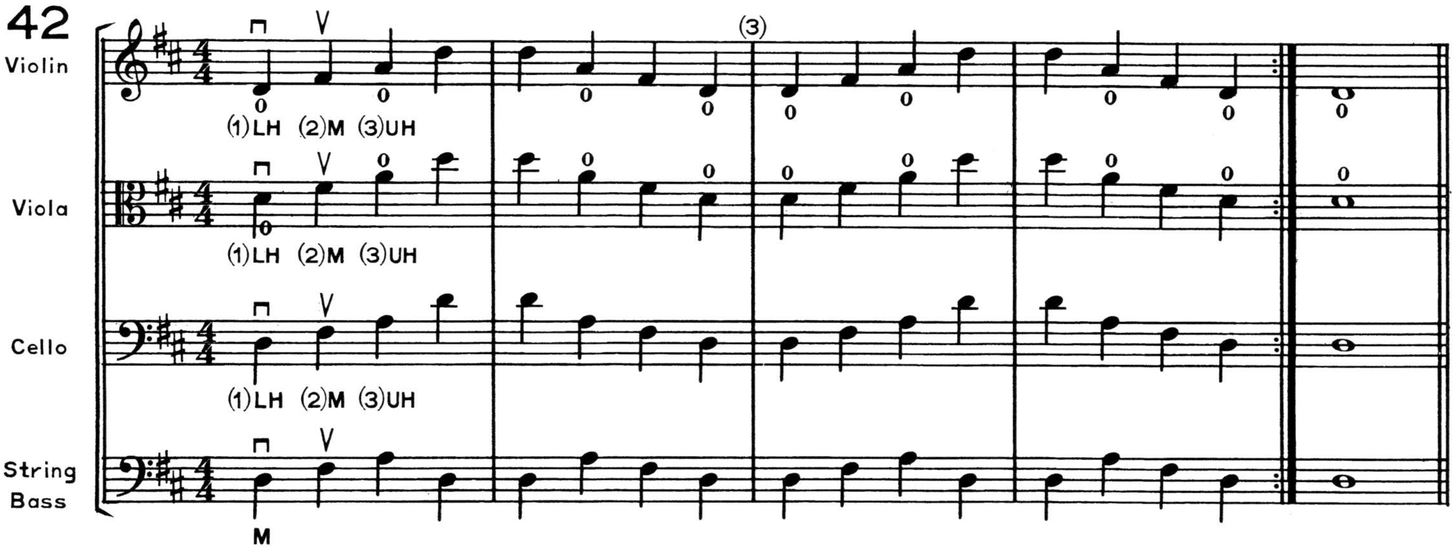

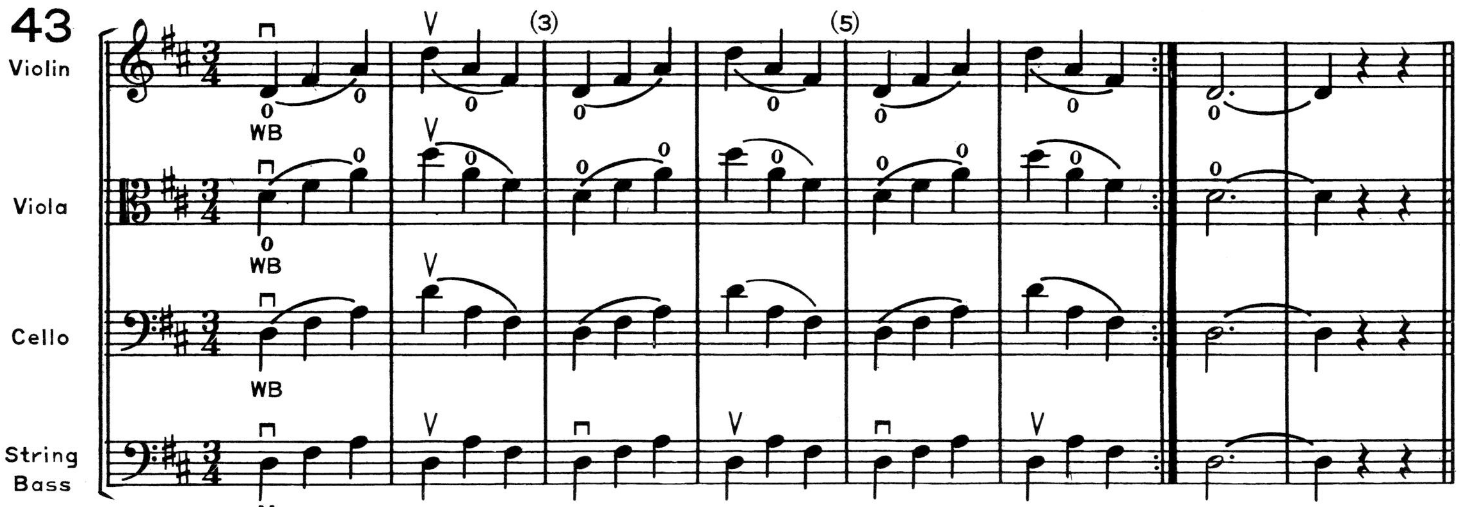

Tone Study

Also practice very slowly, sustaining each tone for EIGHT counts.

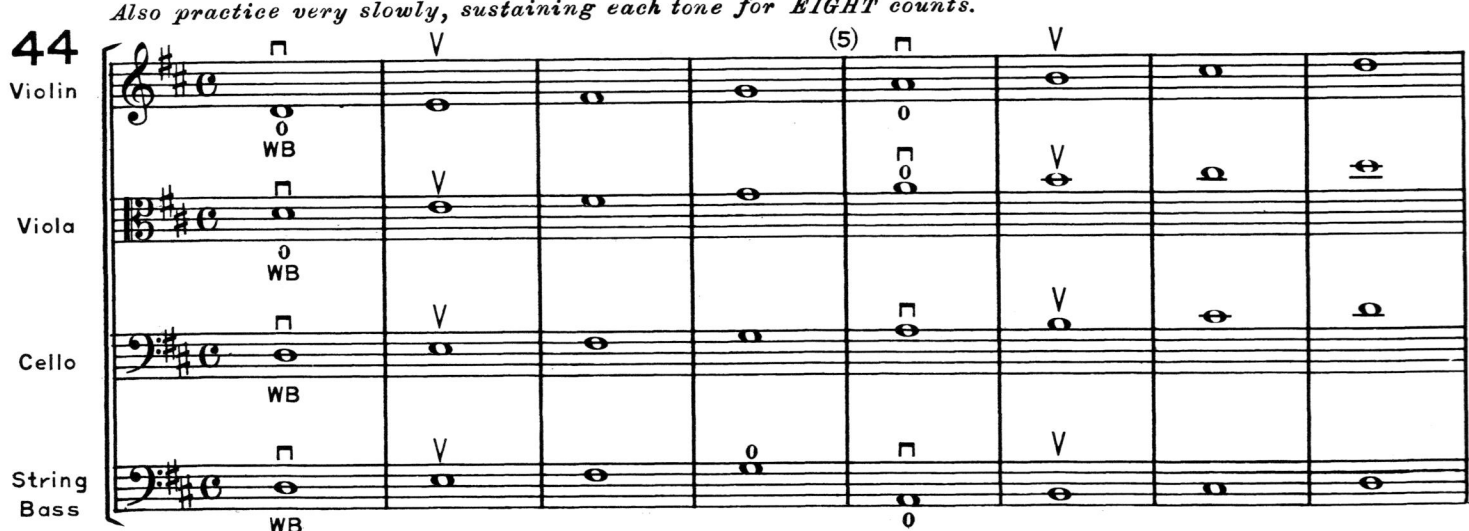

Eighth Notes

Also practice (1) slurring each TWO notes, and (2) slurring each FOUR notes.

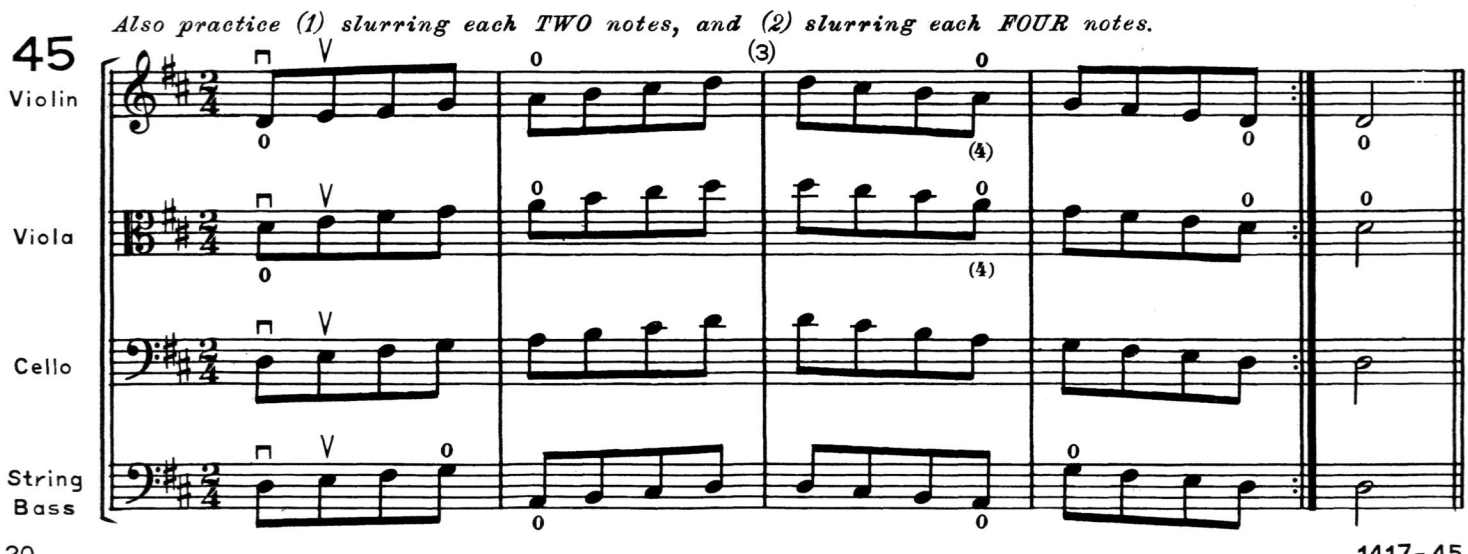

Quarter and Eighth Notes

Key of A Major

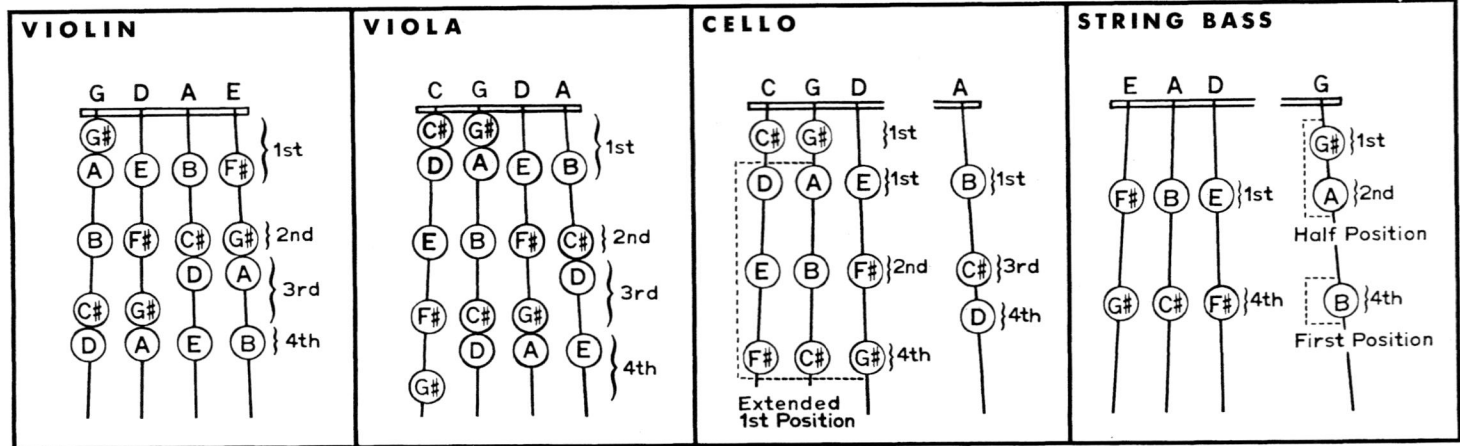

Détaché Scale

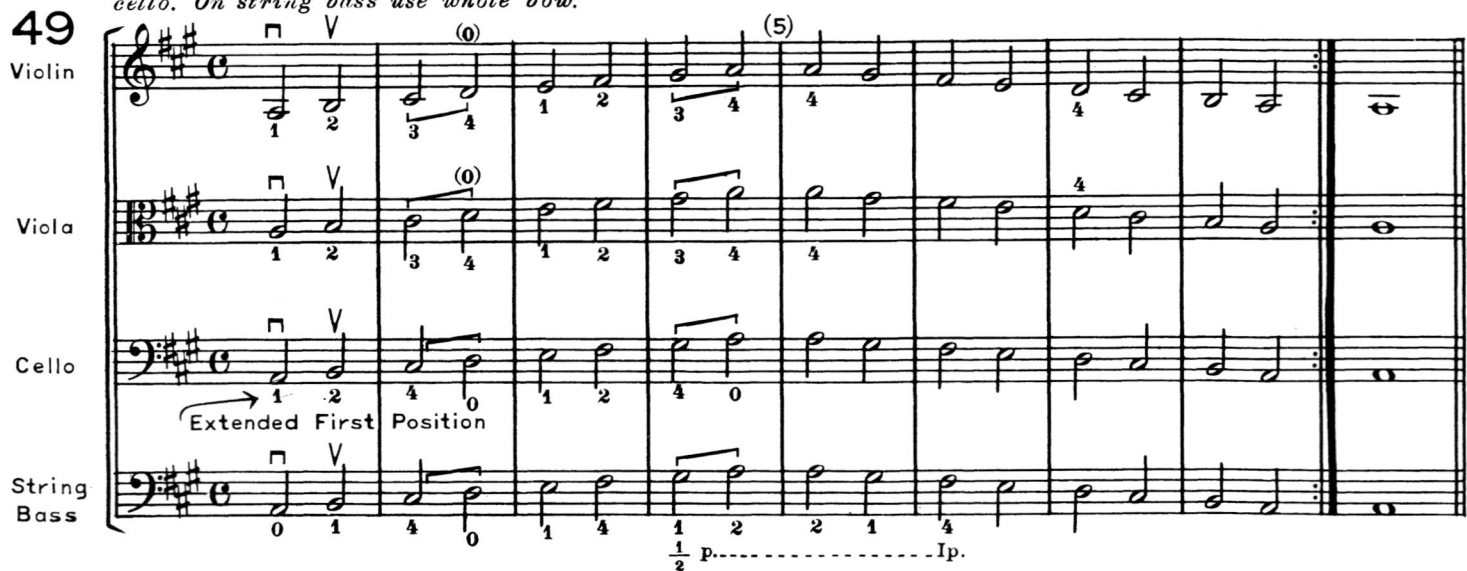

Slurred Scales

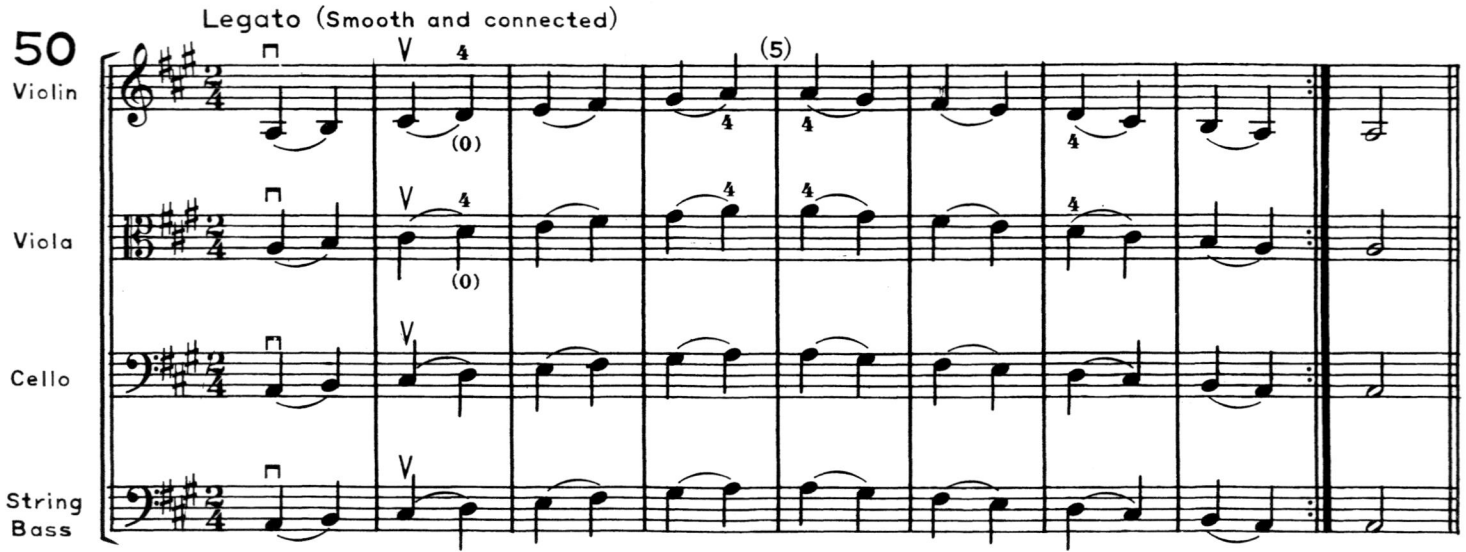

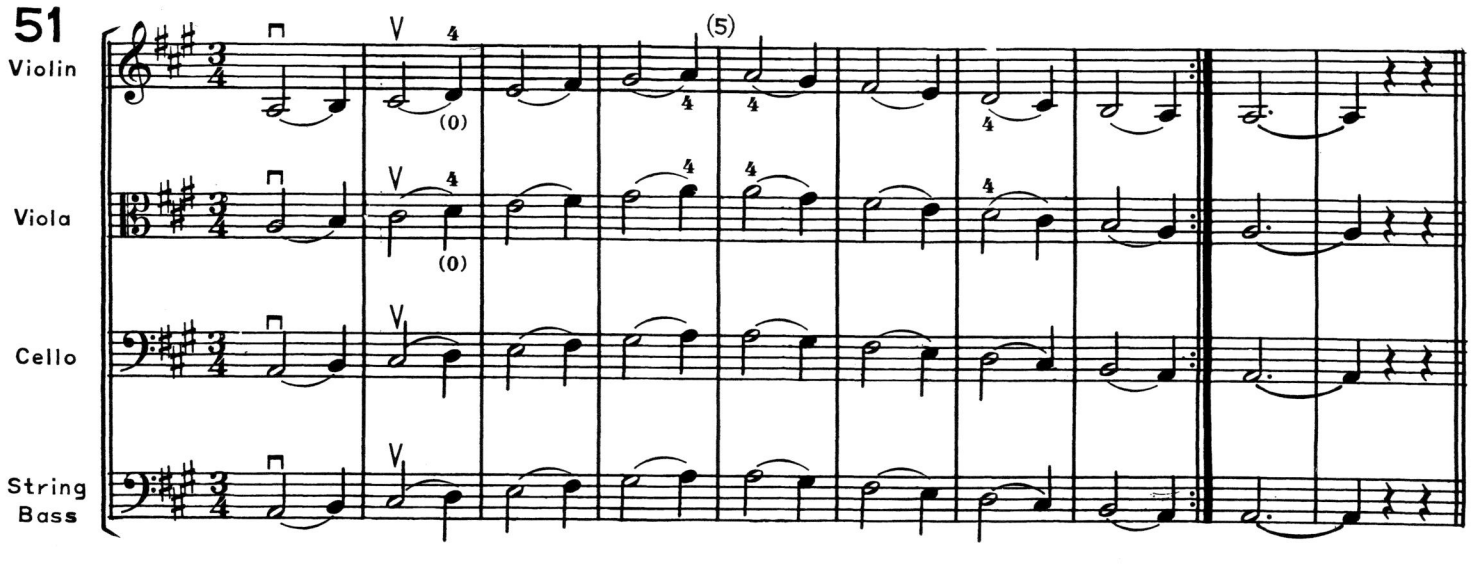

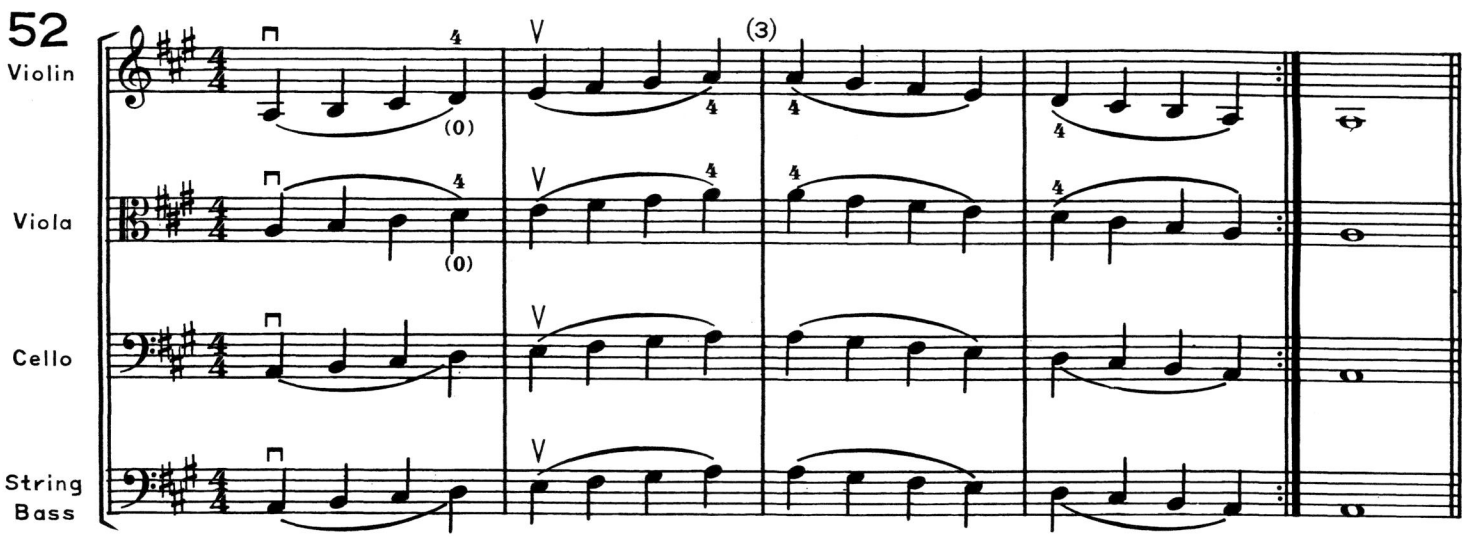

Detached Bowings

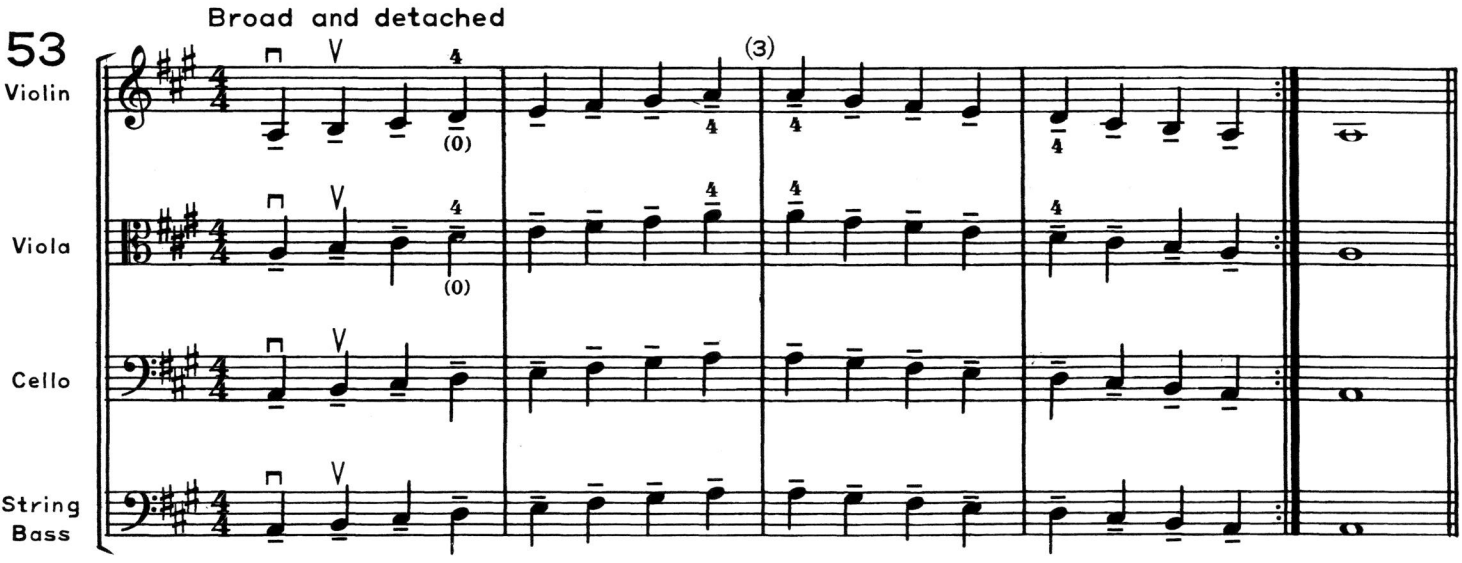

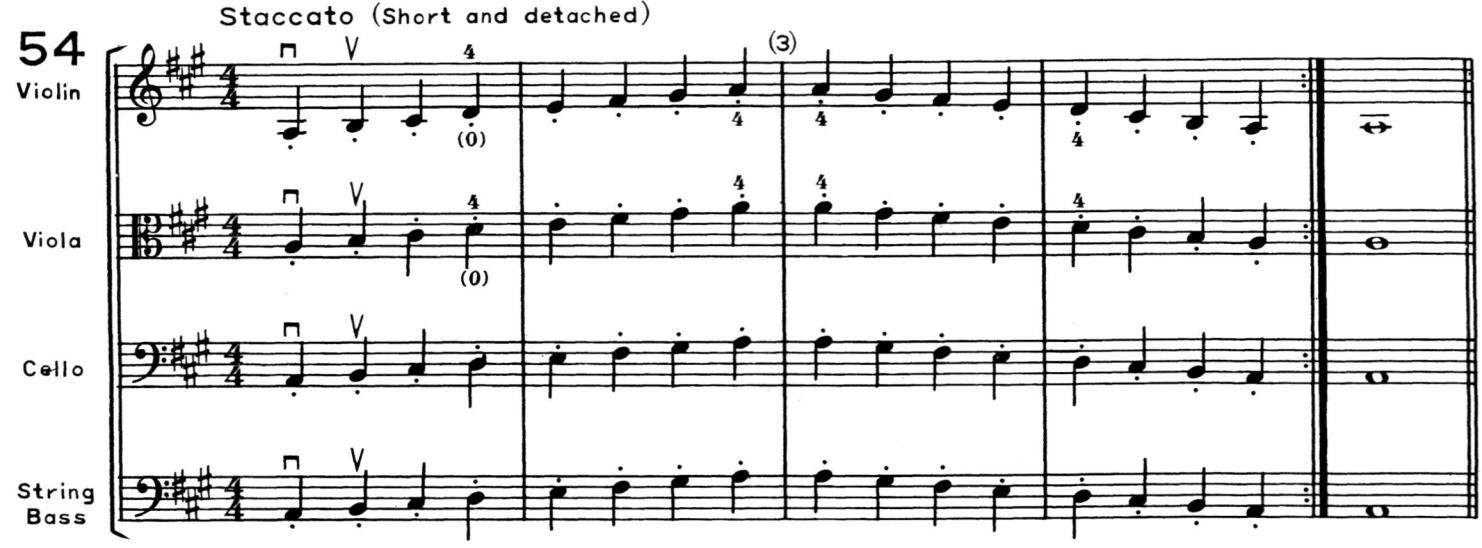

Bow Division

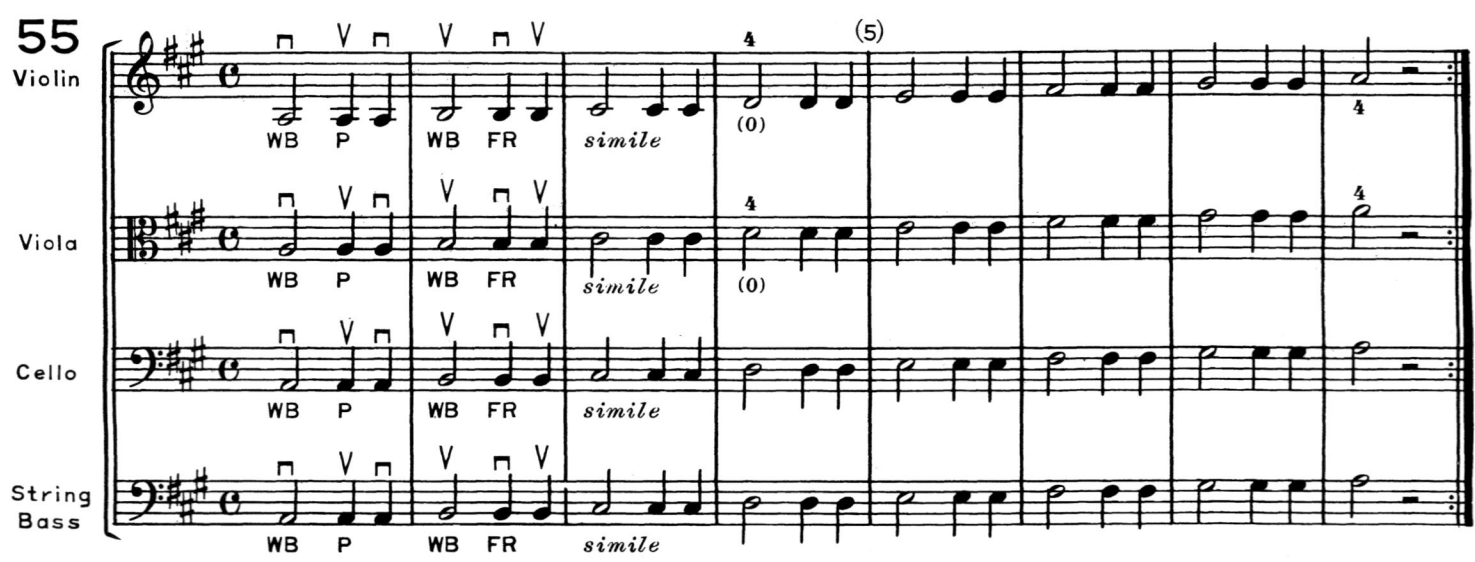

Détaché Scale in Quarter Notes

Use détaché bowing in (1) LOWER HALF, (2) MIDDLE, and (3) UPPER HALF of bow on violin, viola, and cello. On string bass use whole bow.

Broken Chords

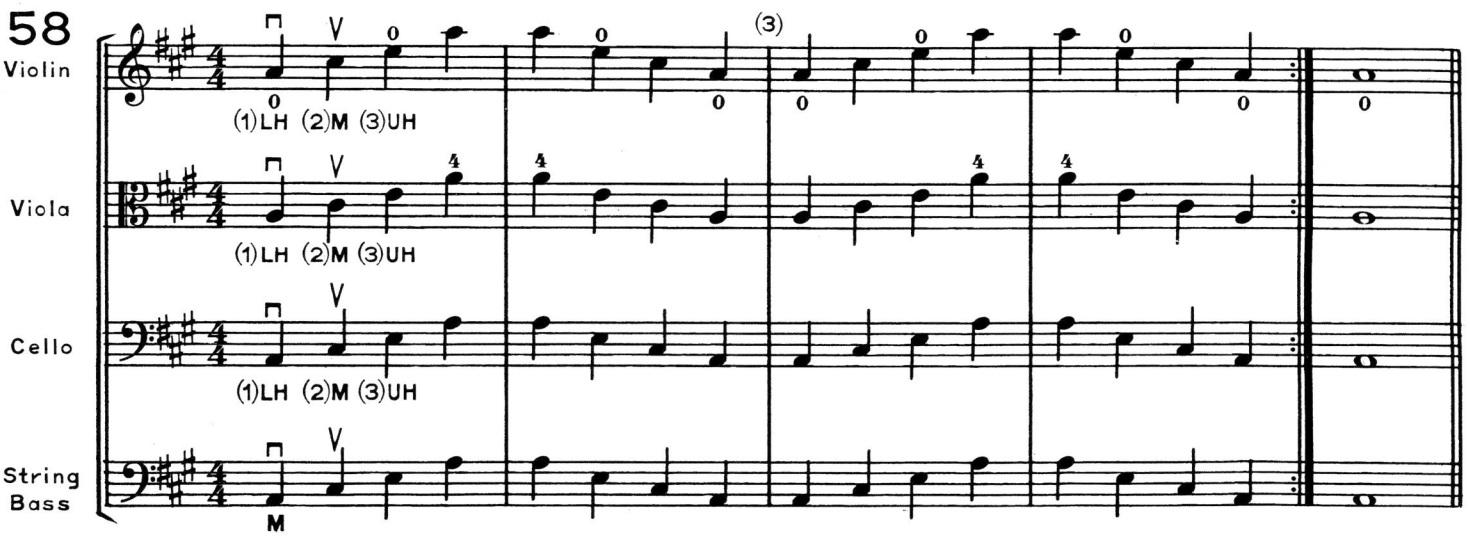

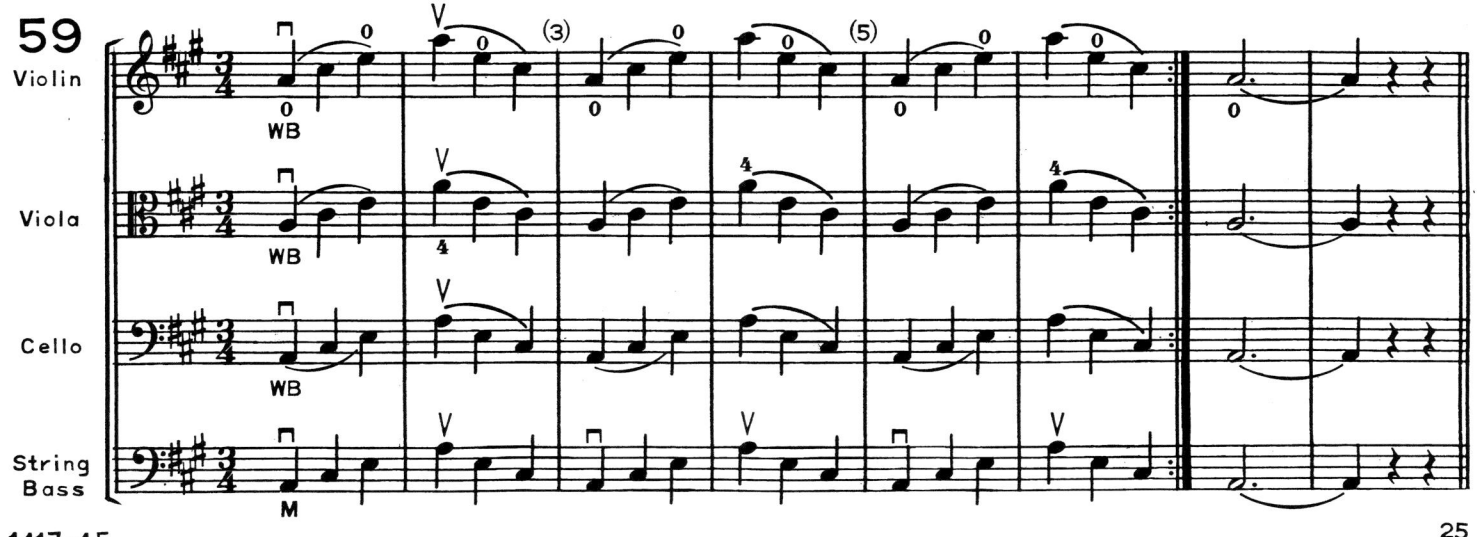

Tone Study

Also practice very slowly, sustaining each tone for EIGHT counts.

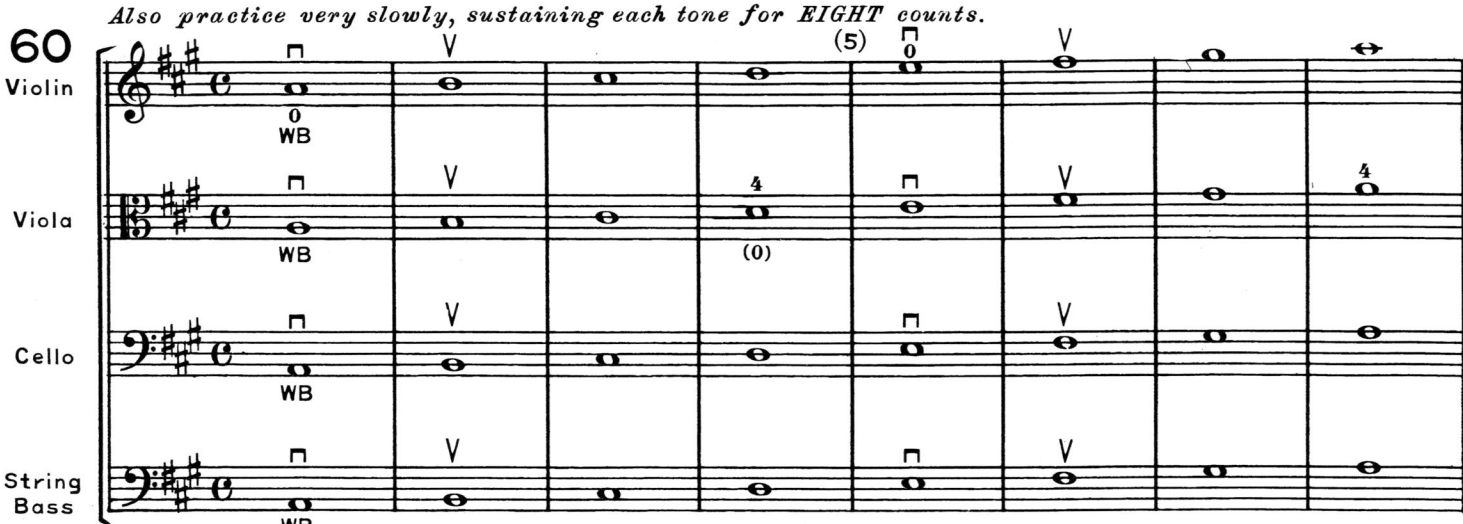

Eighth Notes

Also practice (1) slurring each TWO notes, and (2) slurring each FOUR notes.

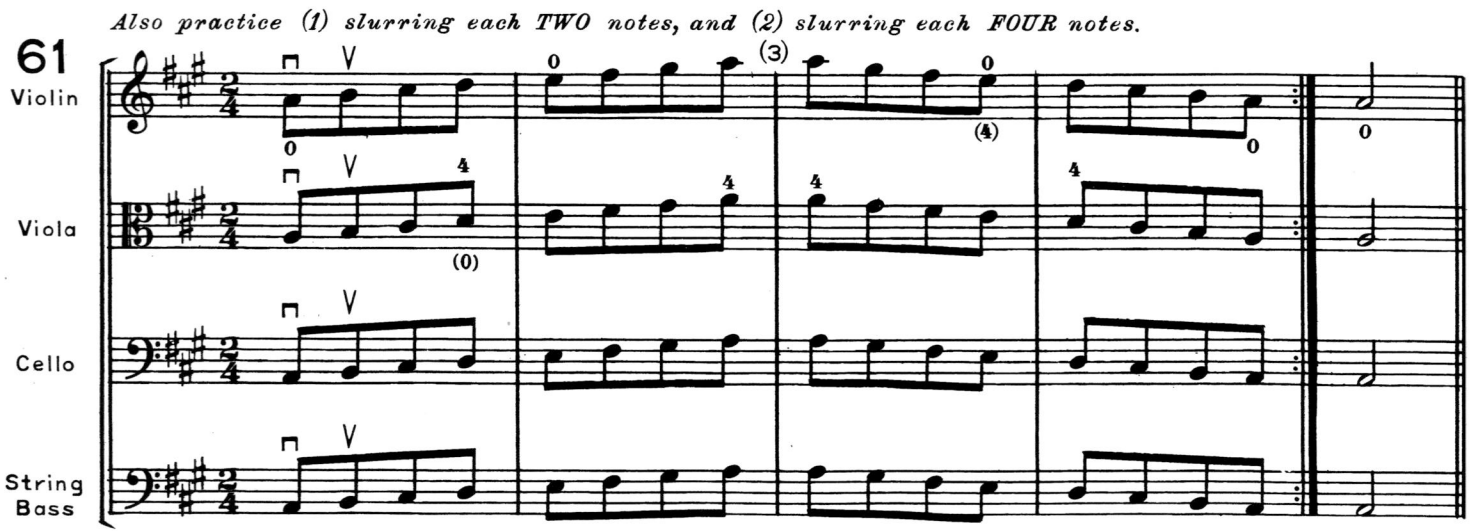

Quarter and Eighth Notes

Key of F Major

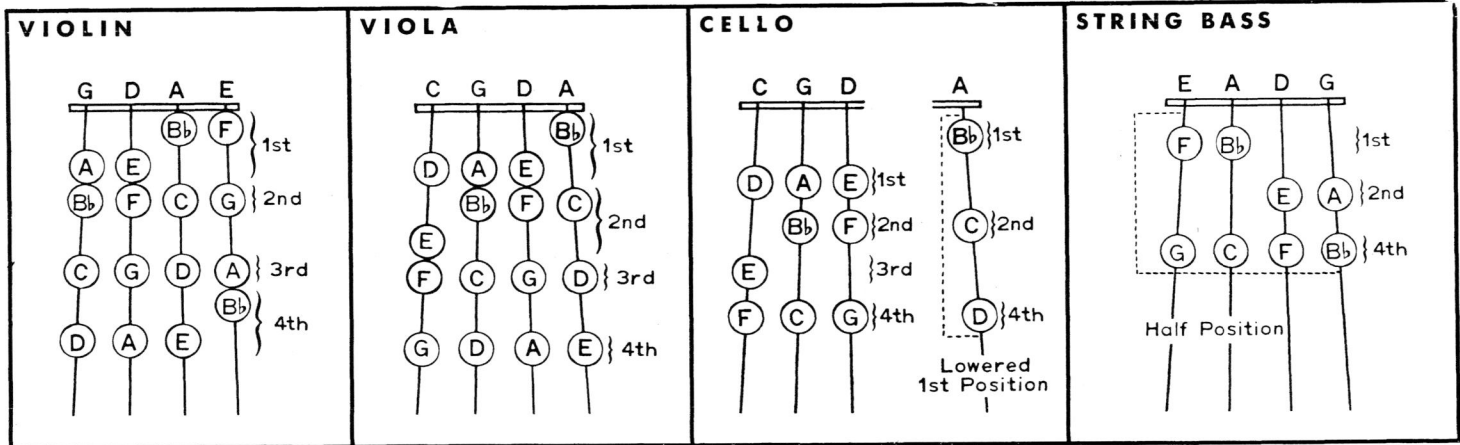

Détaché Scale

Slurred Scales

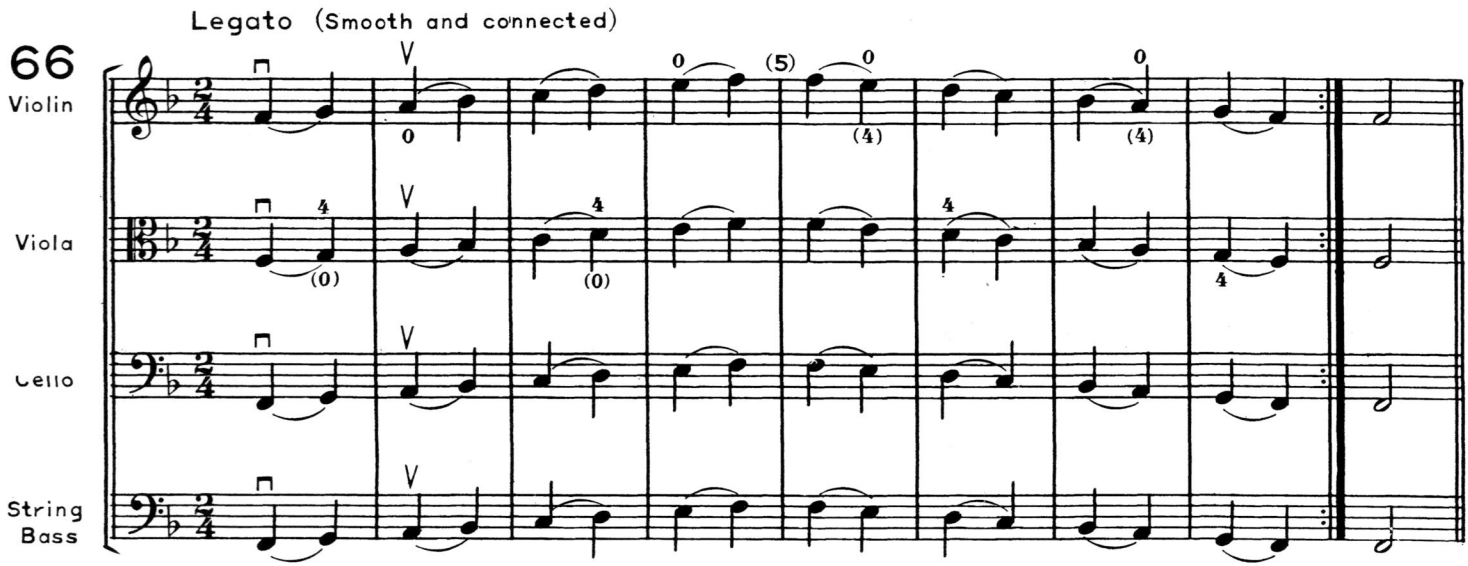

67

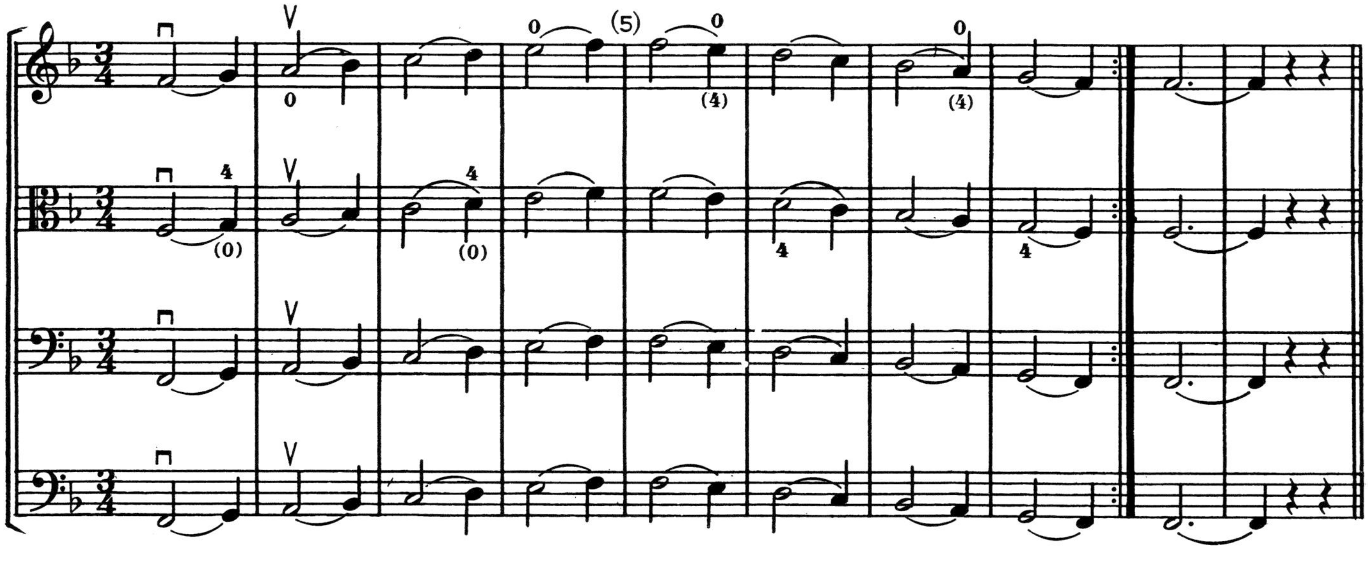

68

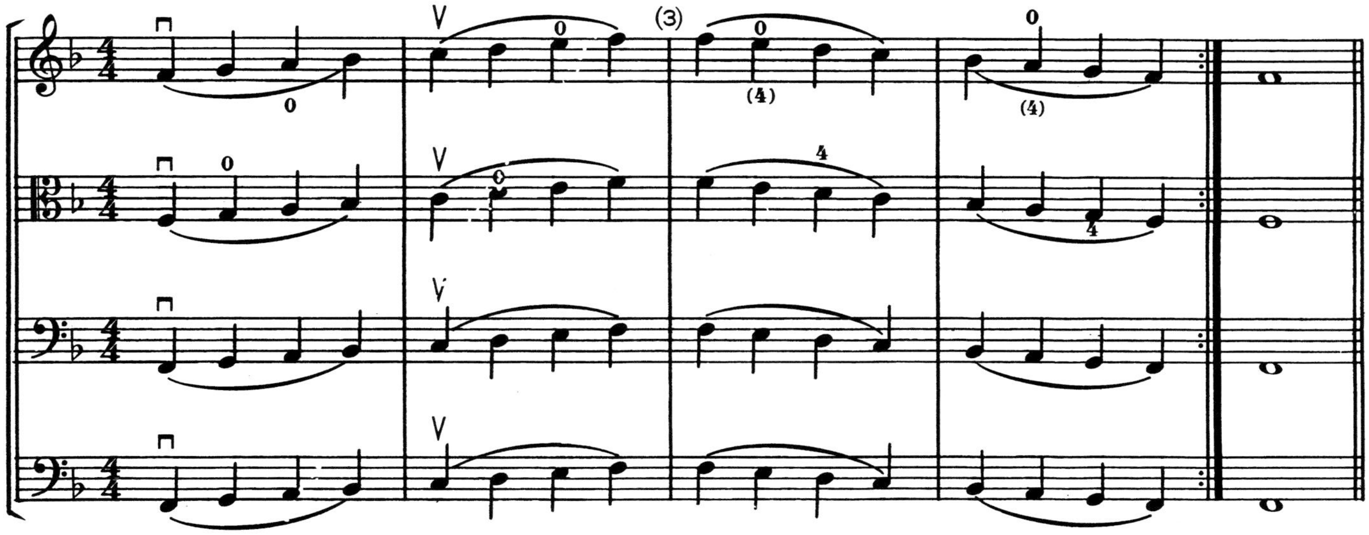

Detached Bowings

Broad and detached

69

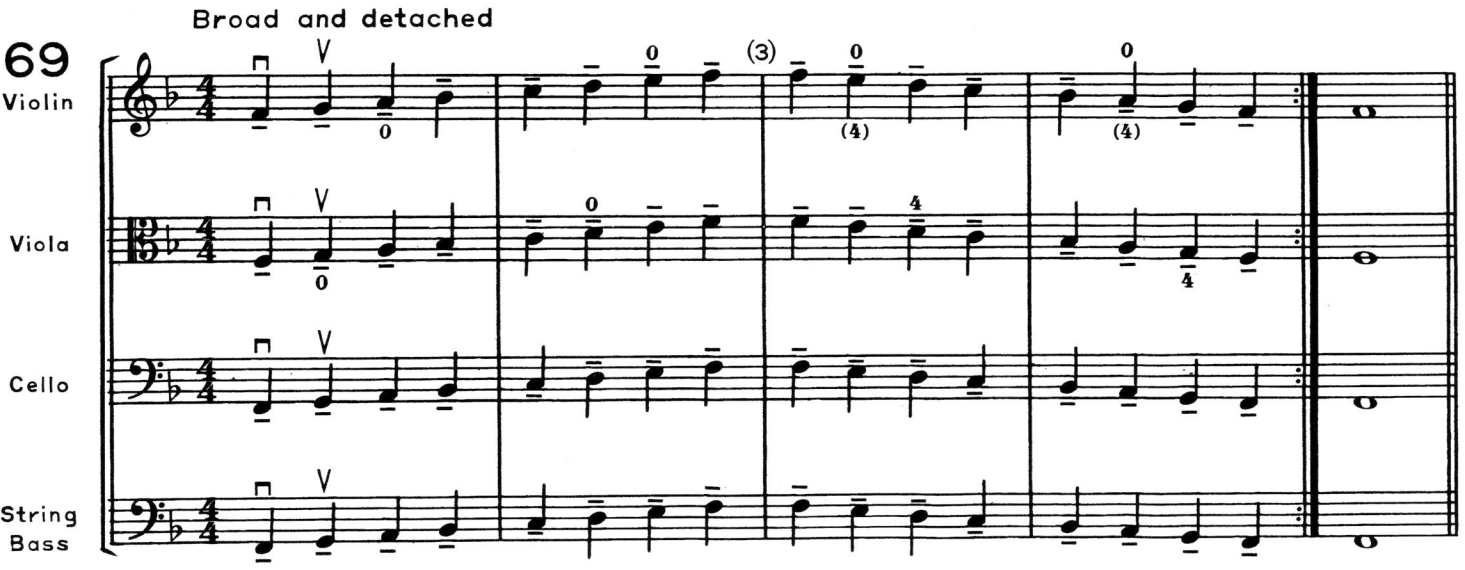

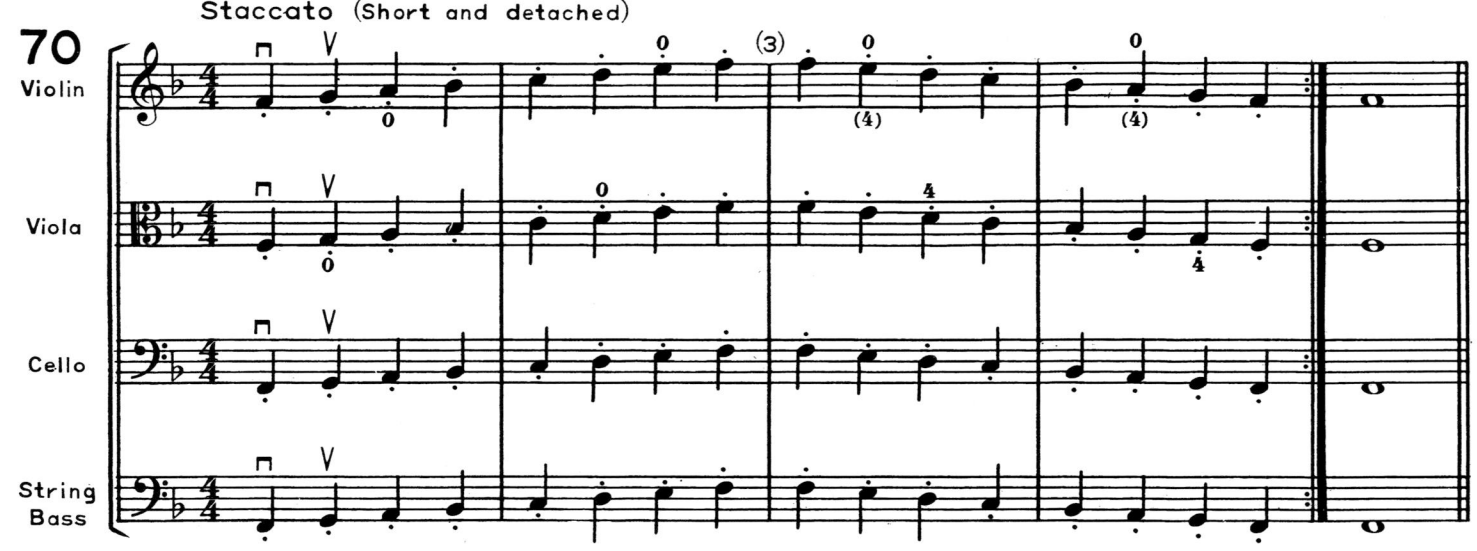

Bow Division

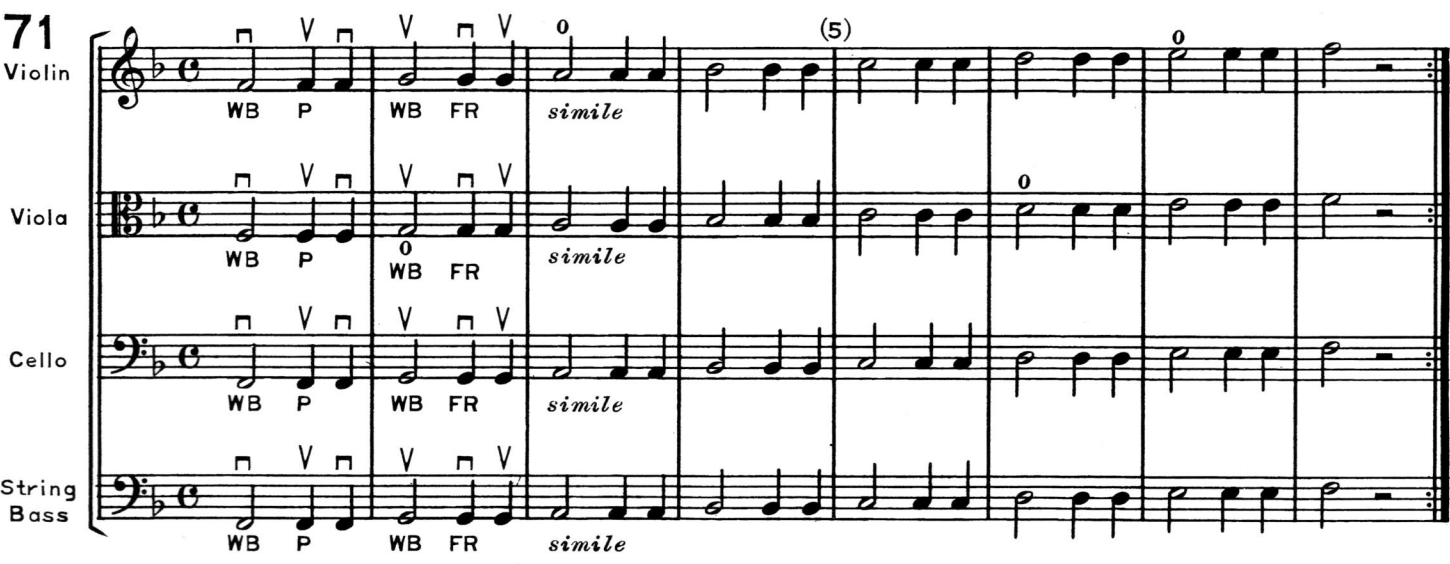

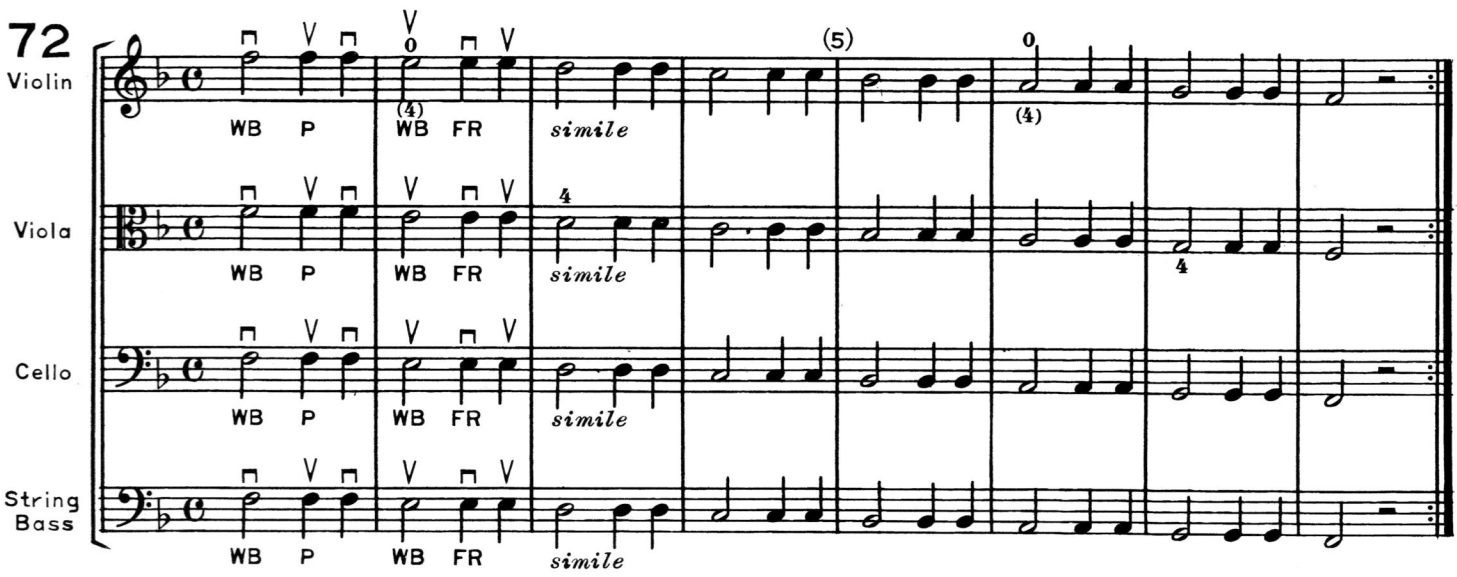

Détaché Scale in Quarter Notes

Use détaché bowing in (1) LOWER HALF, (2) MIDDLE, and (3) UPPER HALF of bow for violin, viola, and cello. On string bass use whole bow.

Broken Chords

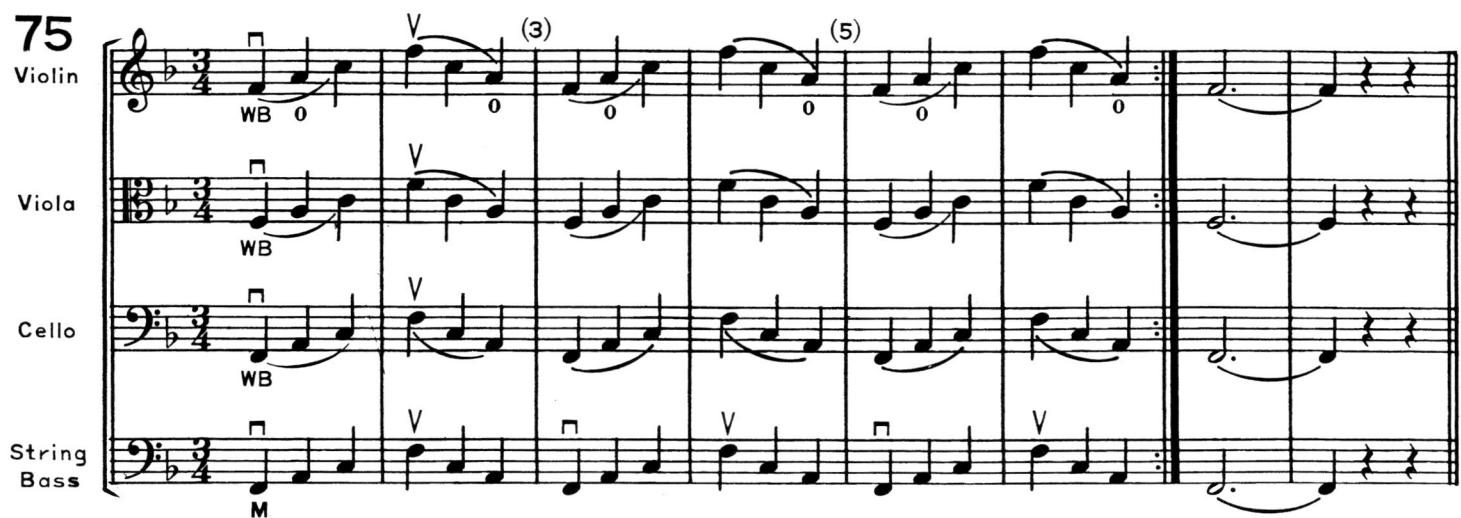

Tone Study

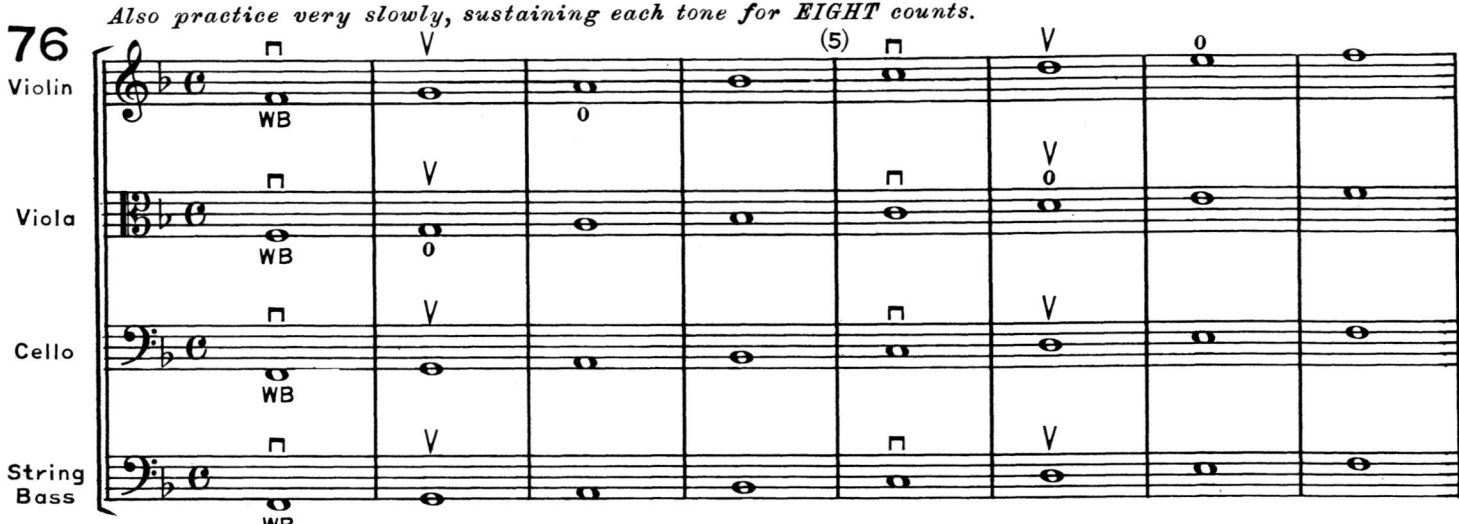

Eighth Notes

Quarter and Eighth Notes

Key of B♭ Major

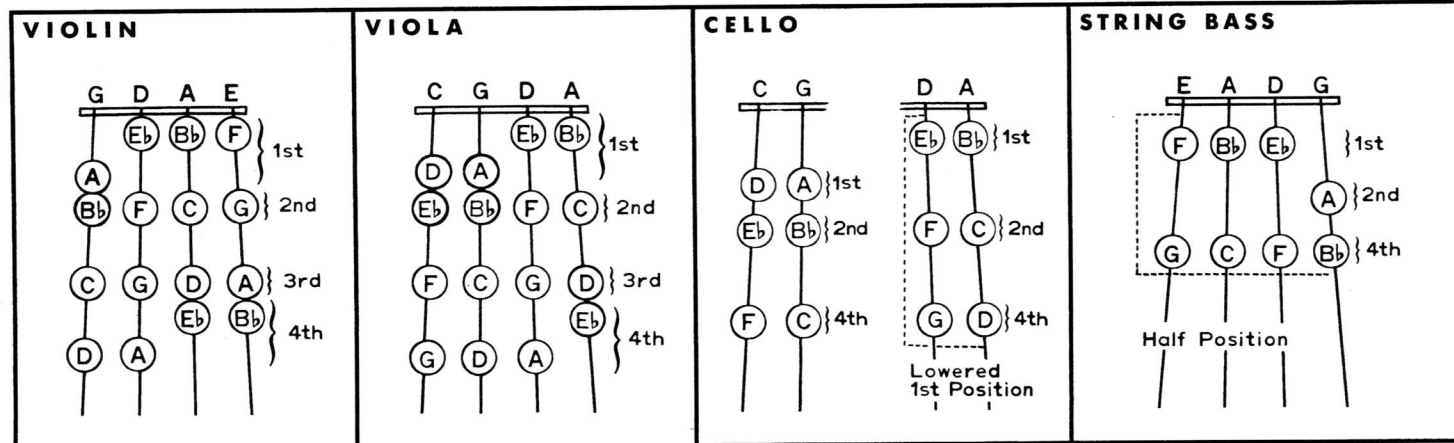

Détaché Scale

Slurred Scales

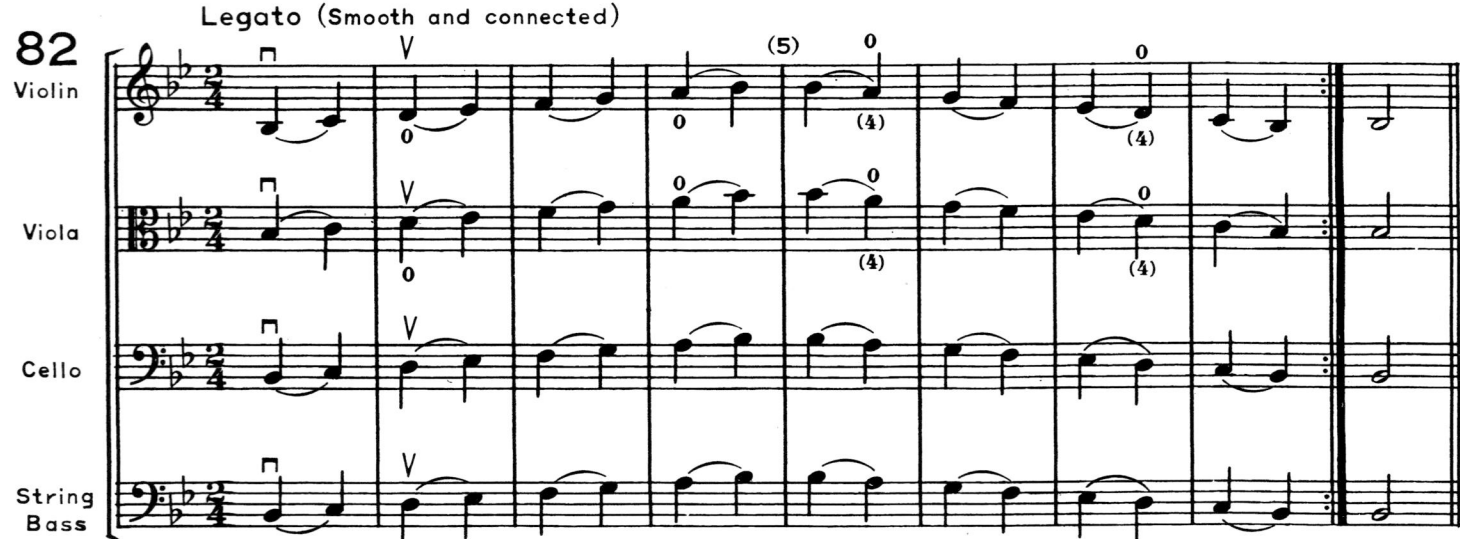

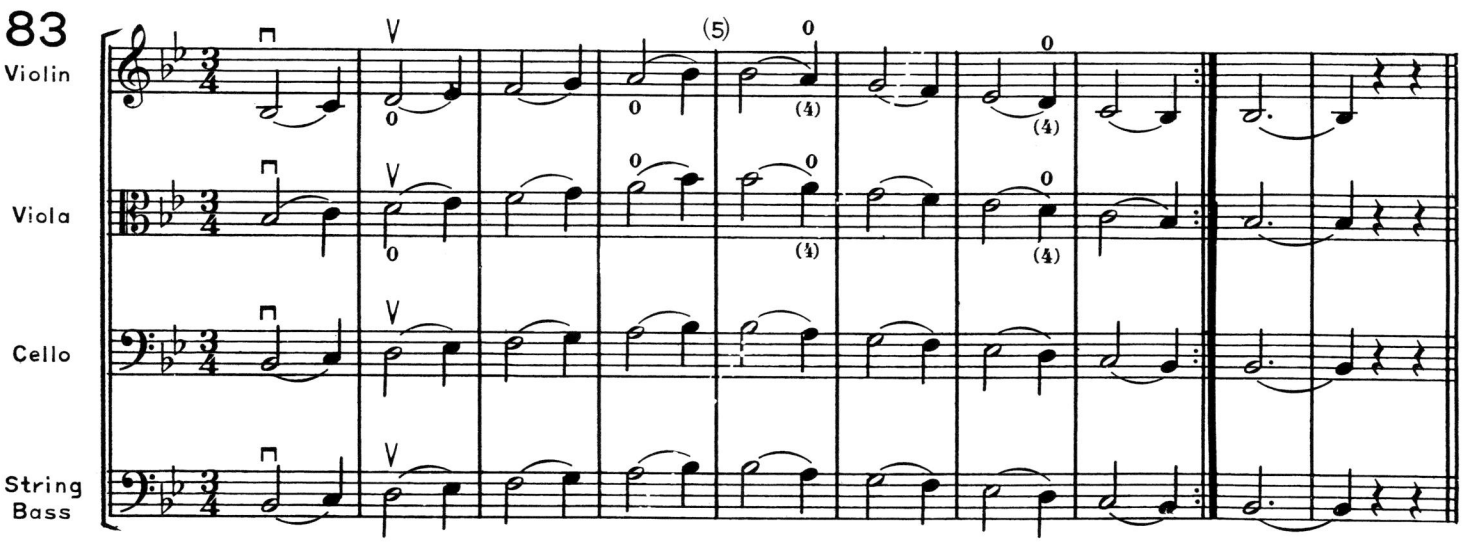

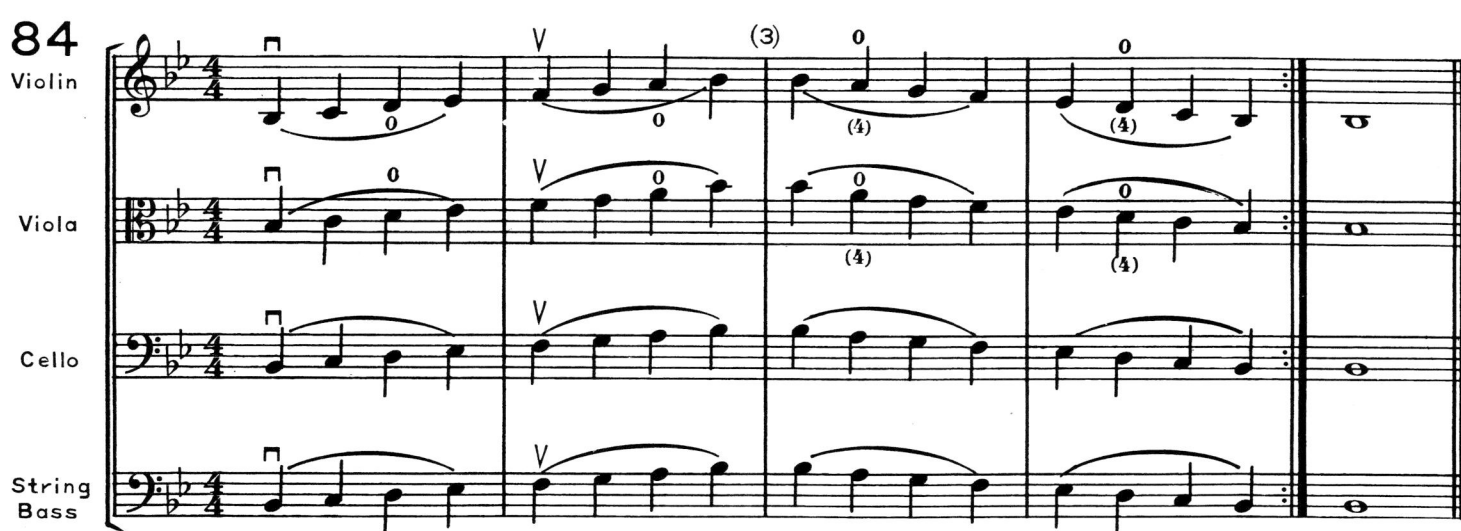

Detached Bowings

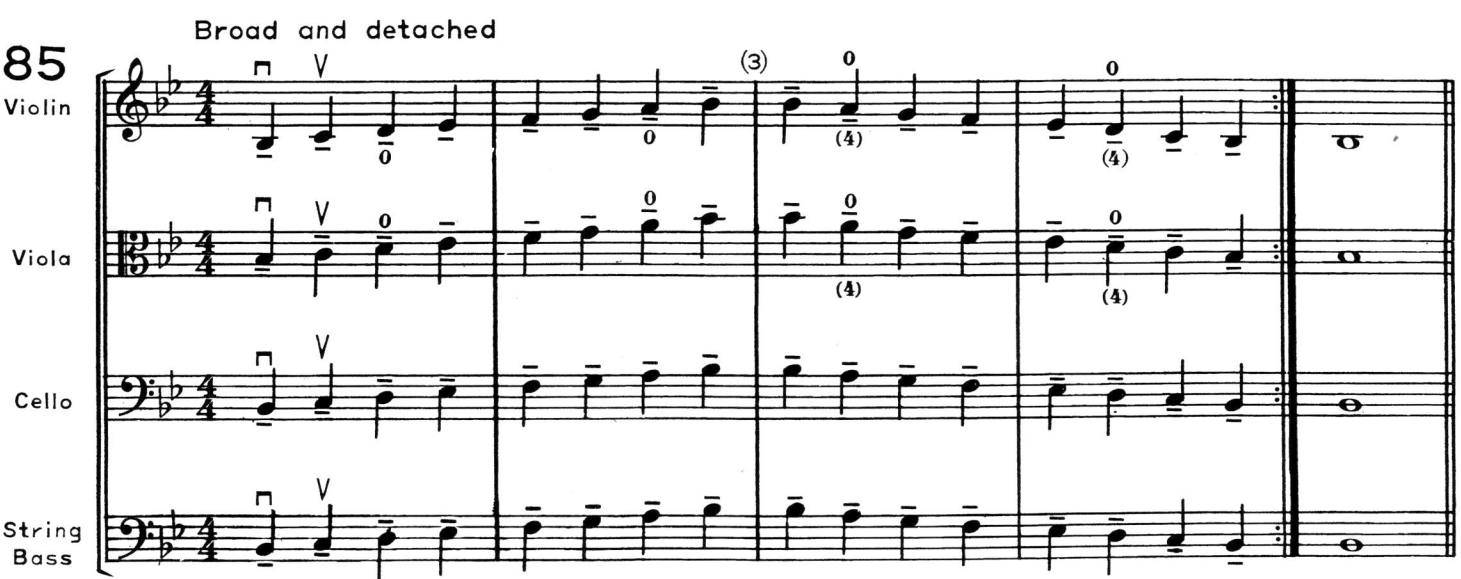

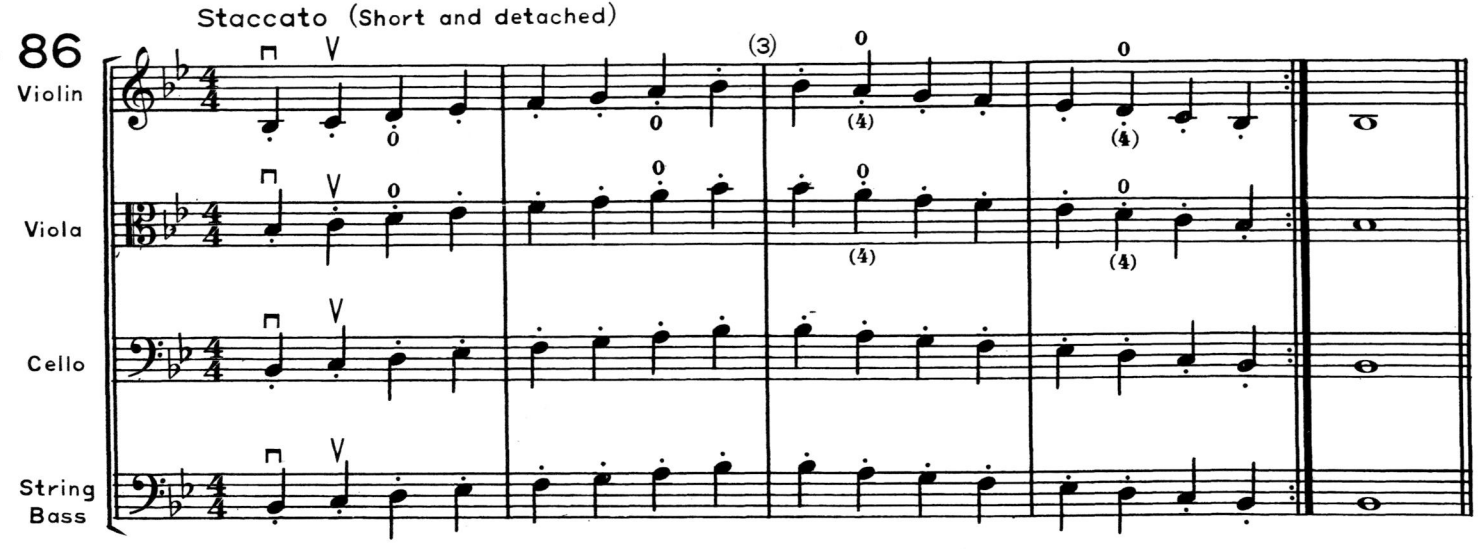

Bow Division

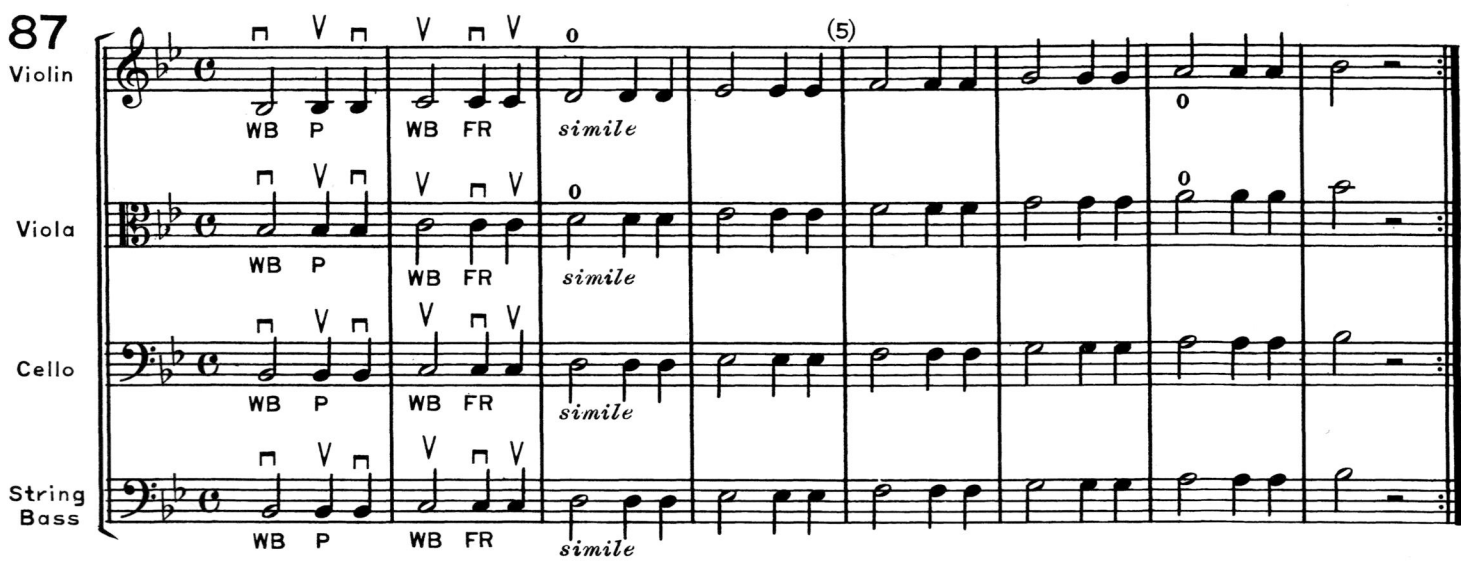

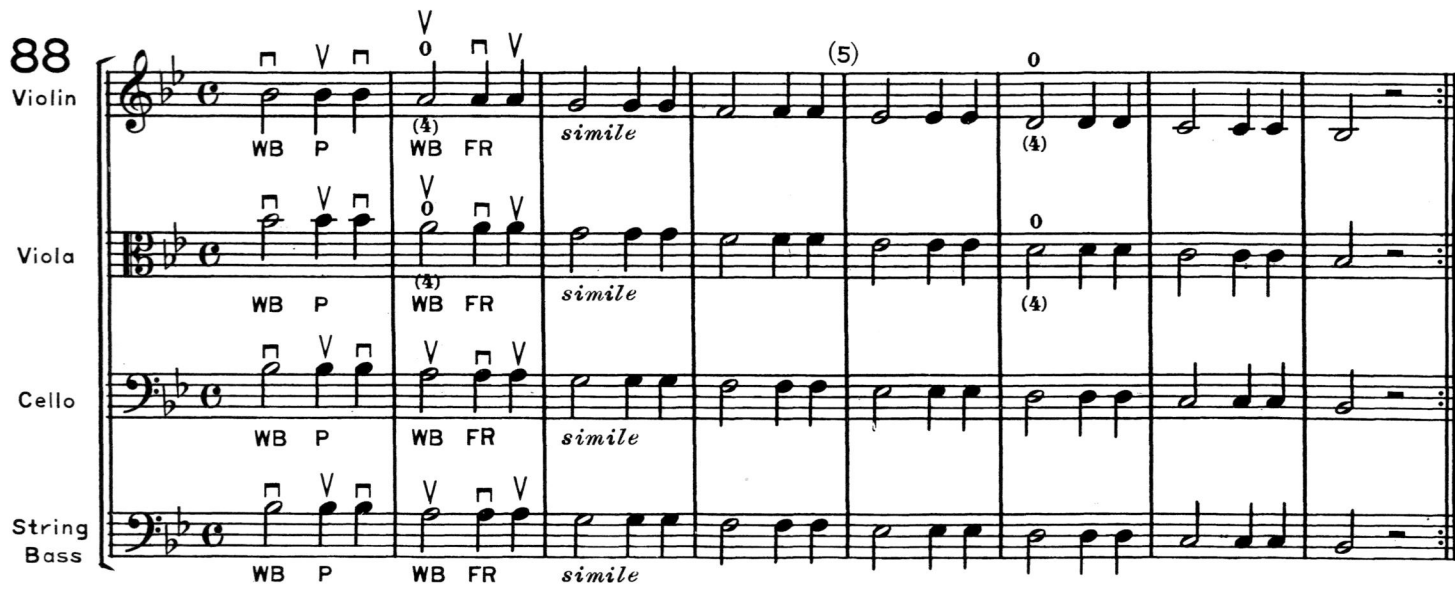

Détaché Scale in Quarter Notes

Use détaché bowing in (1) LOWER HALF, (2) MIDDLE, and (3) UPPER HALF of bow on violin, viola, and cello. On string bass use whole bow.

Broken Chords

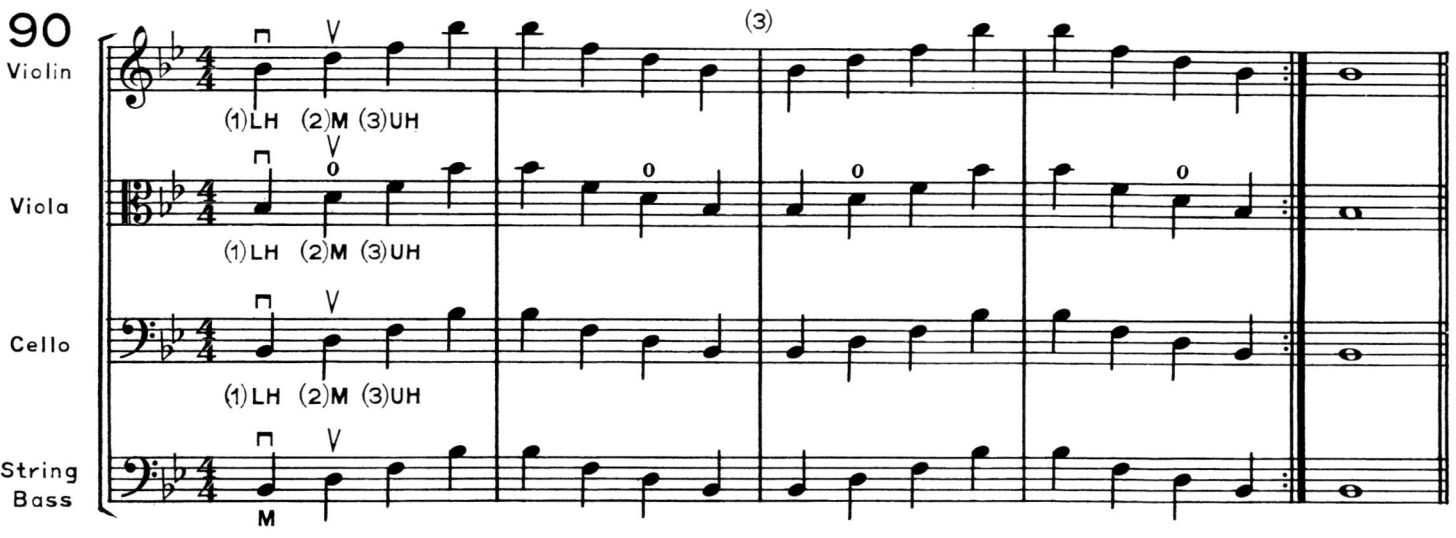

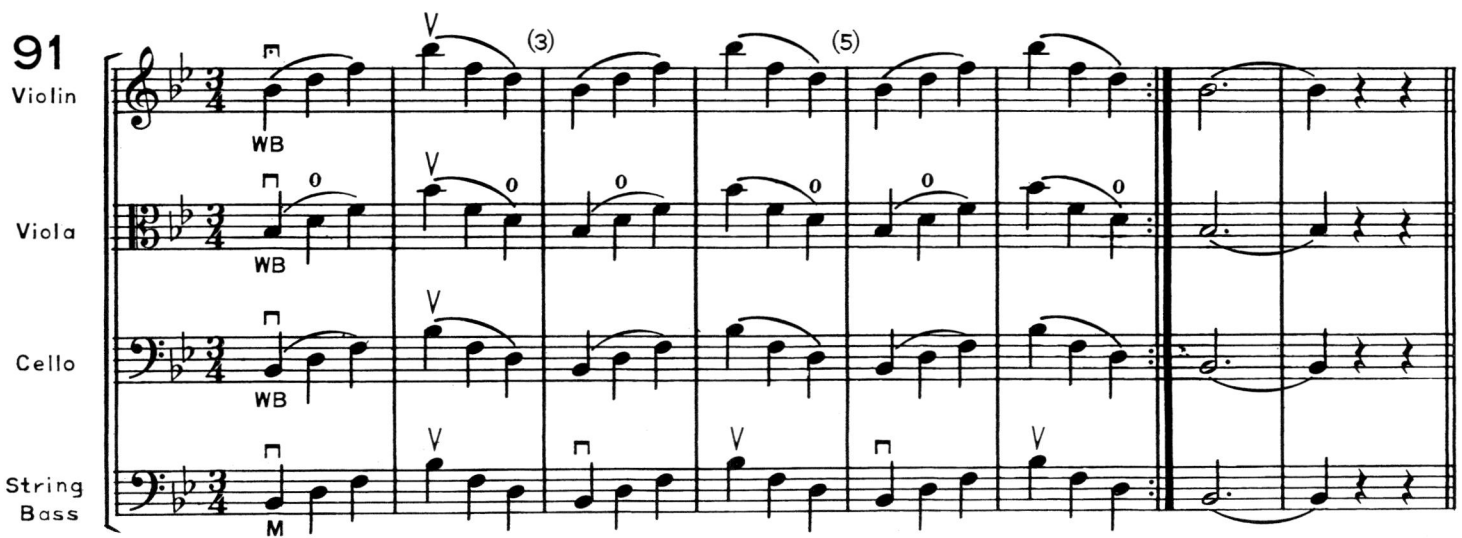

Tone Study

Also practice very slowly, sustaining each tone for EIGHT counts.

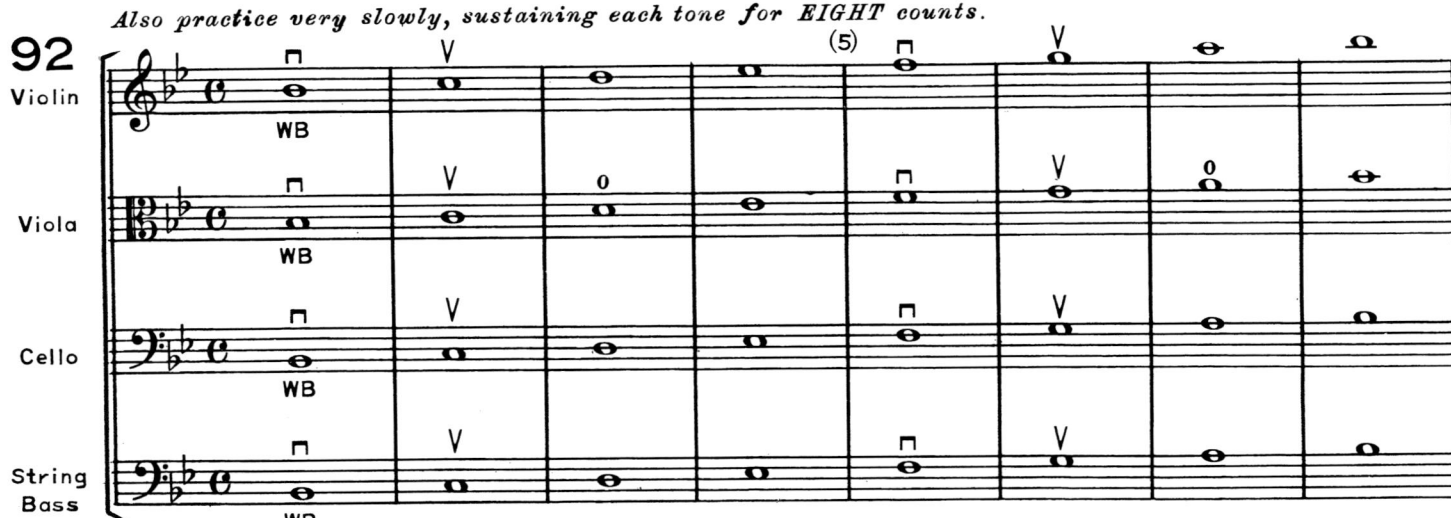

Eighth Notes

Also practice (1) slurring each TWO notes, and (2) slurring each FOUR notes.

Quarter and Eighth Notes

Key of E♭ Major

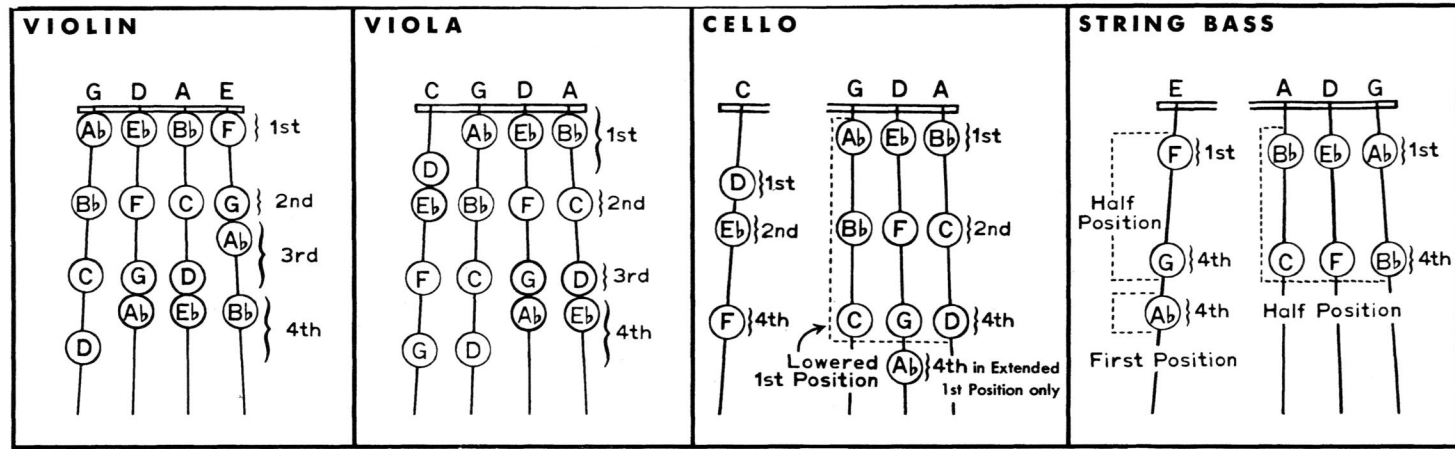

Détaché Scale

Use détaché bowing in (1) LOWER HALF, (2) MIDDLE, and (3) UPPER HALF of bow on violin, viola, and cello. On string bass use whole bow.

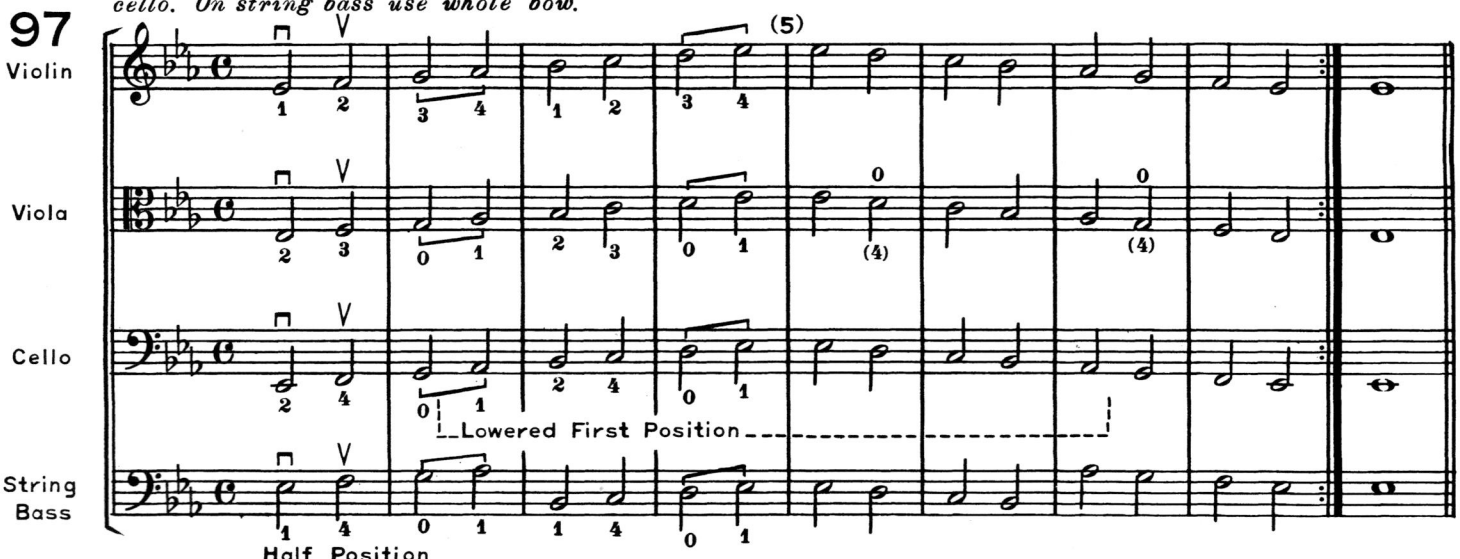

Slurred Scales

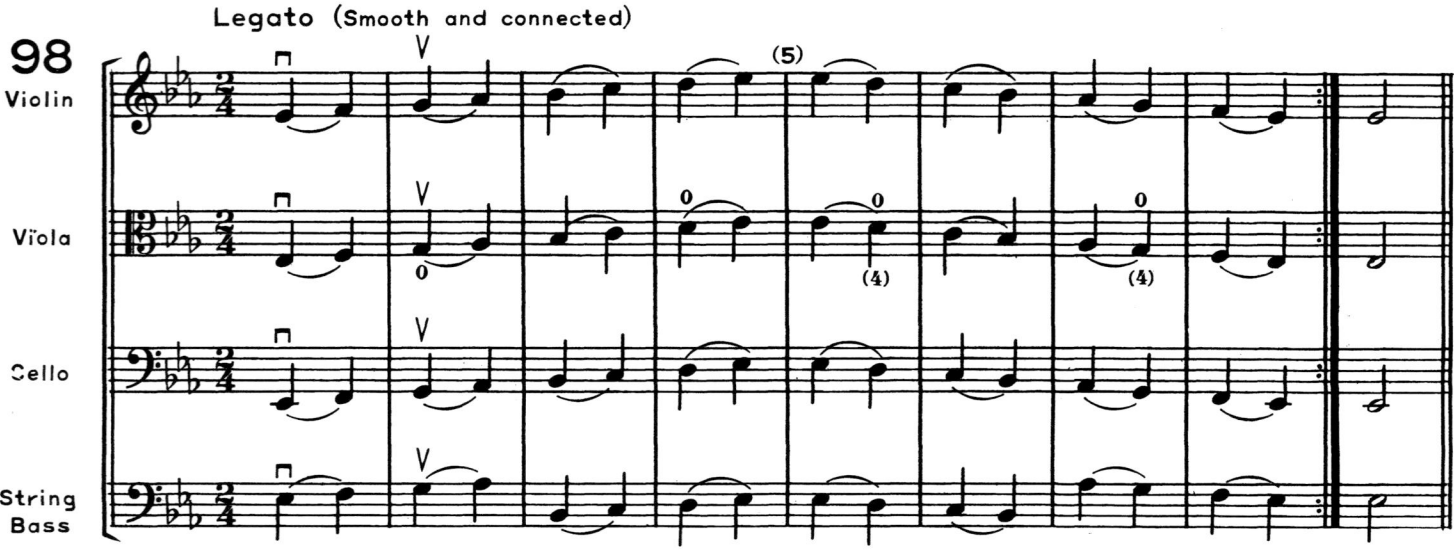

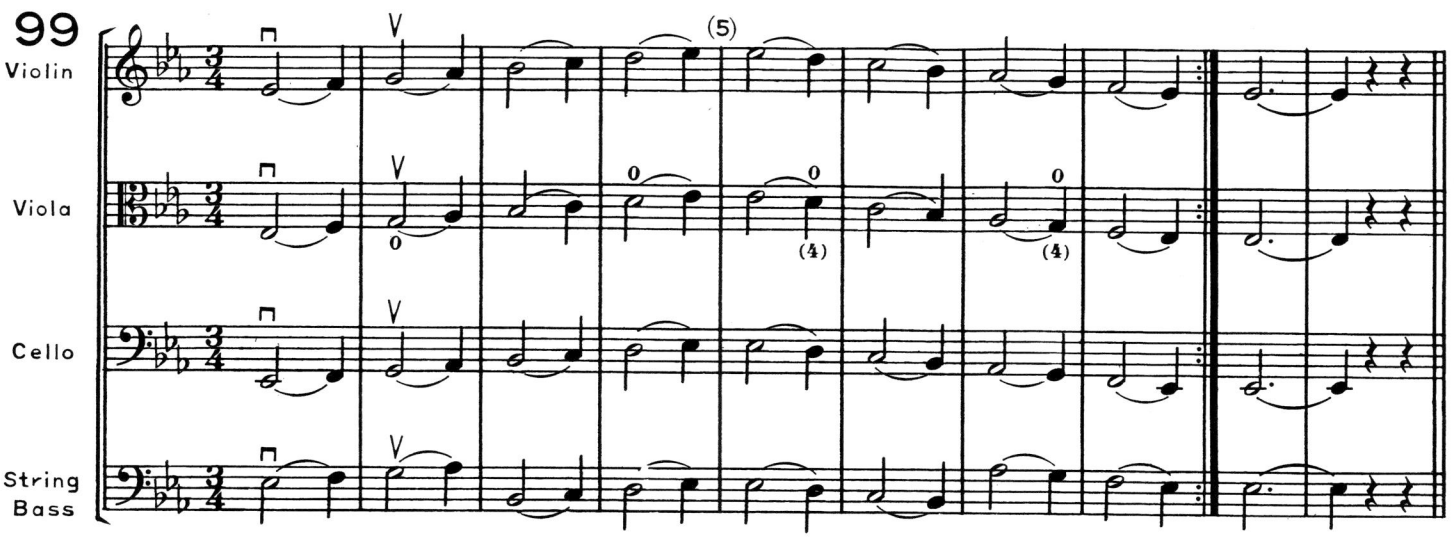

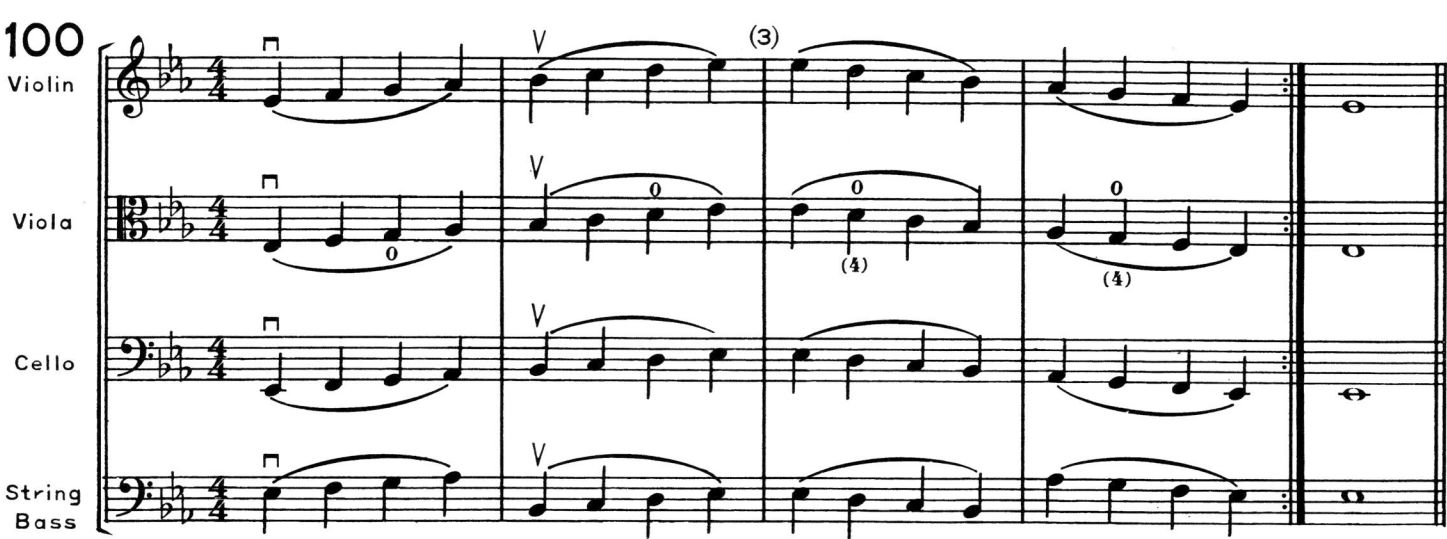

Detached Bowings

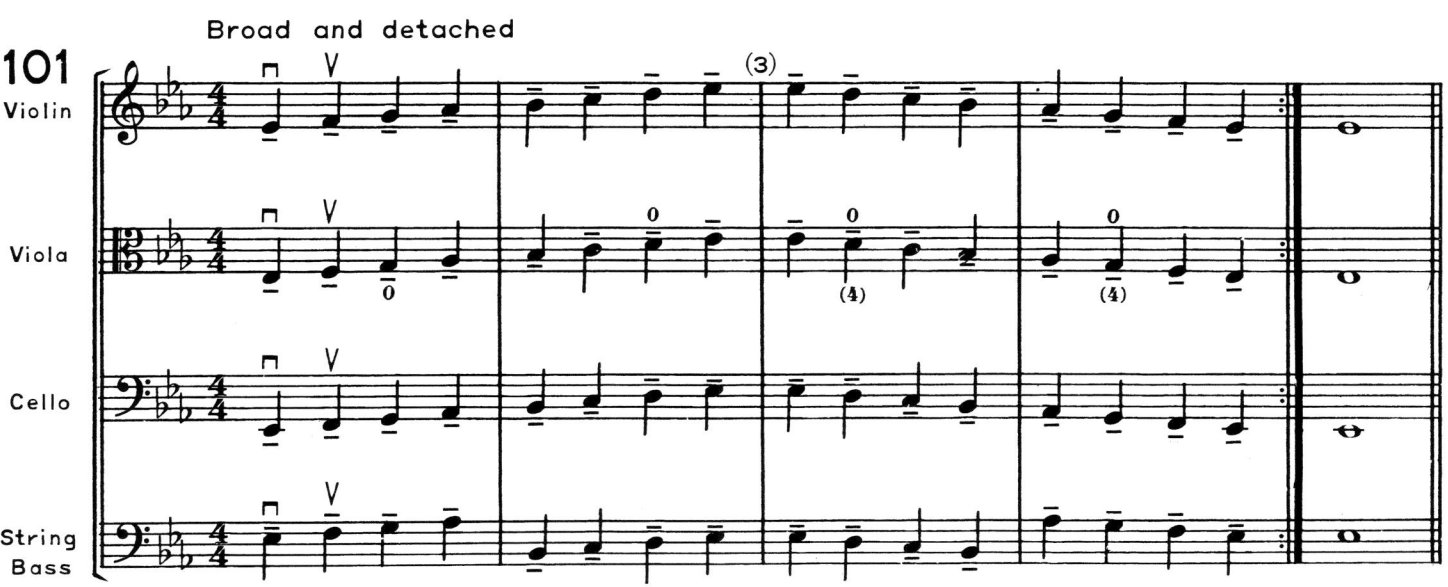

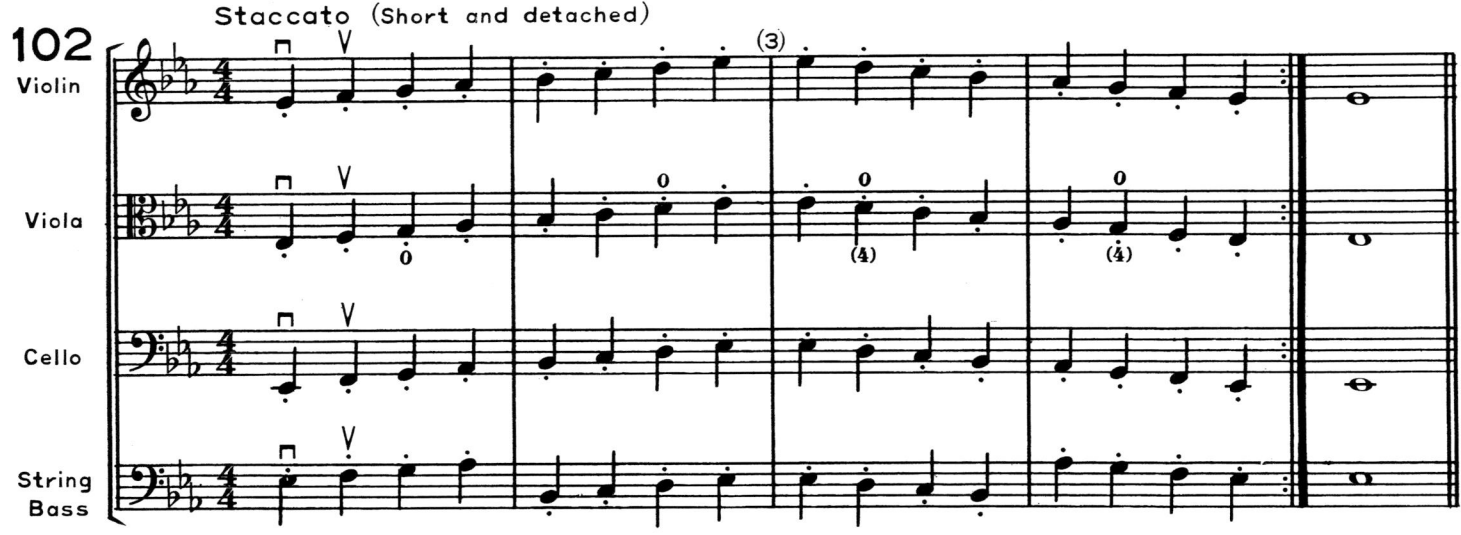

Bow Division

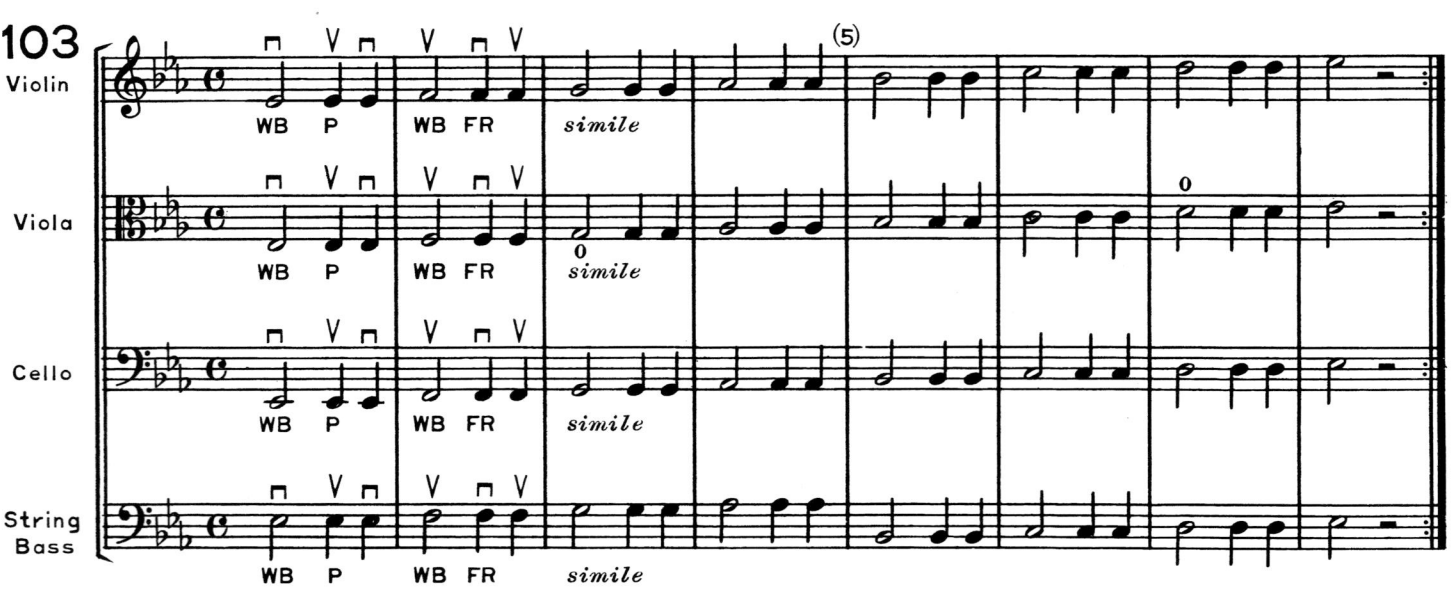

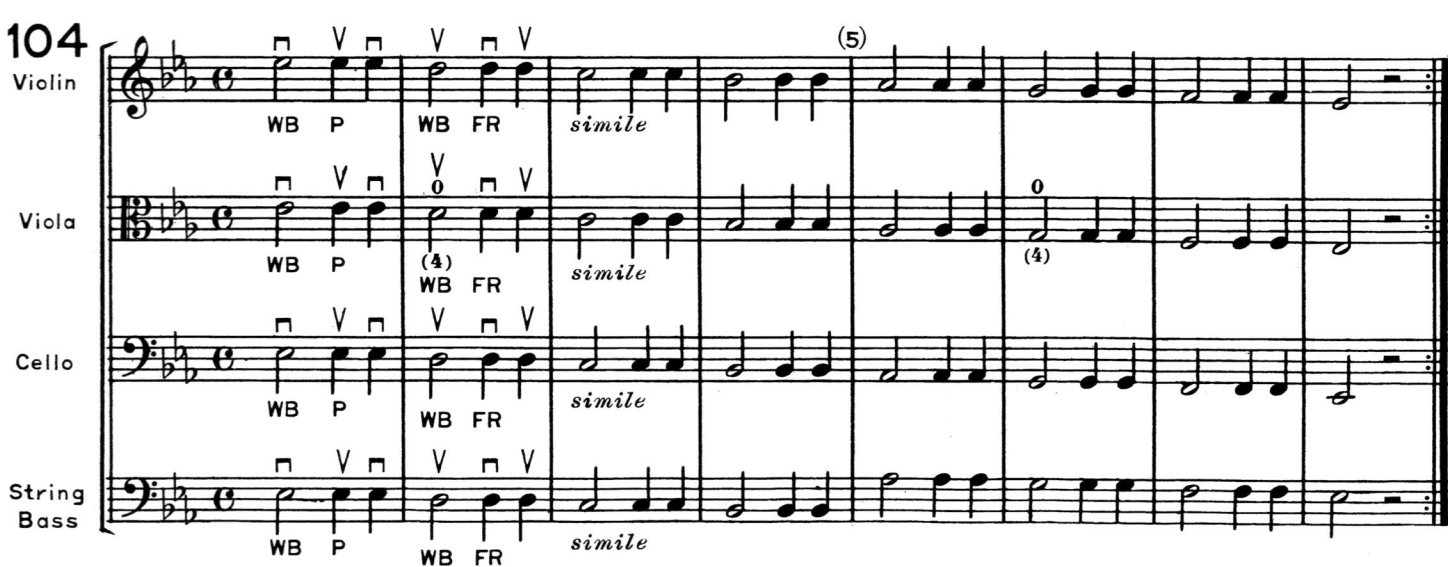

Détaché Scale in Quarter Notes

Use détaché bowing in (1) LOWER HALF, (2) MIDDLE, and (3) UPPER HALF of bow on violin, viola, and cello. On string bass use whole bow.

Broken Chords

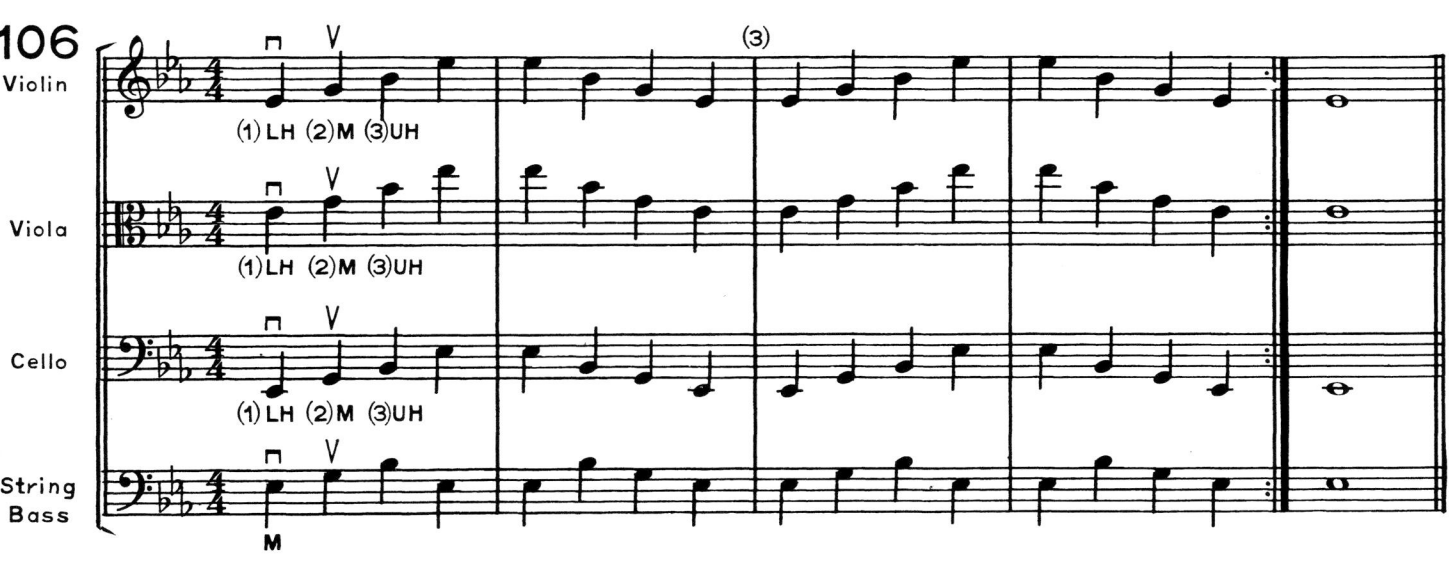

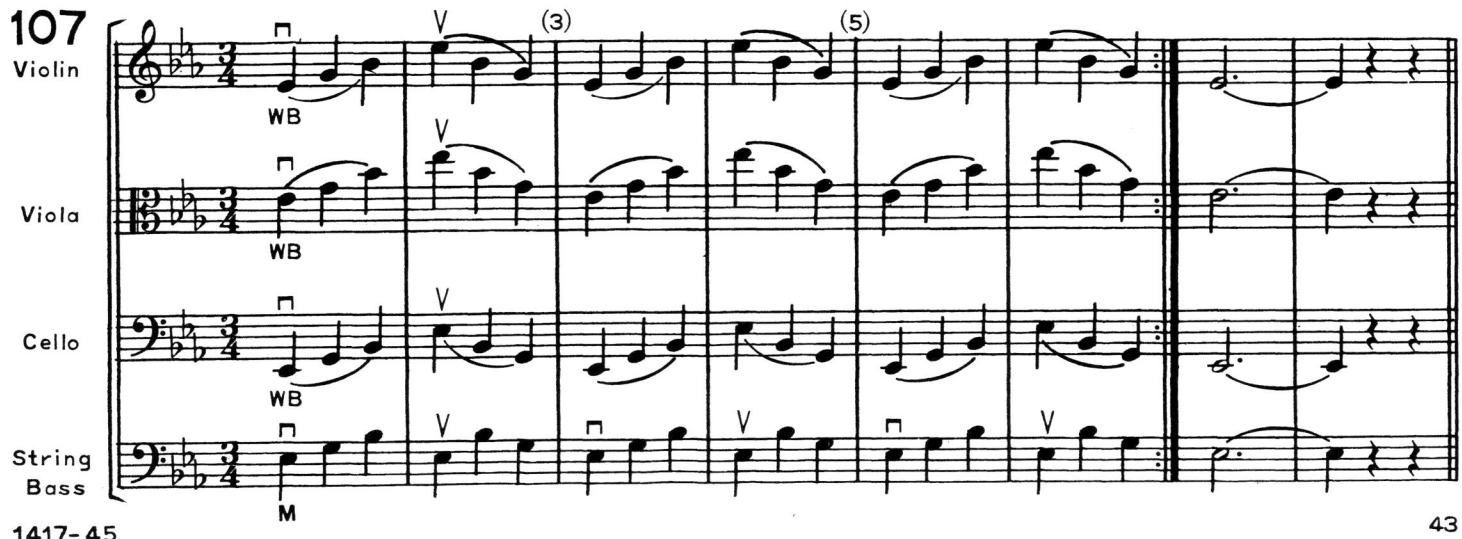

Tone Study

Also practice very slowly, sustaining each tone for EIGHT counts.

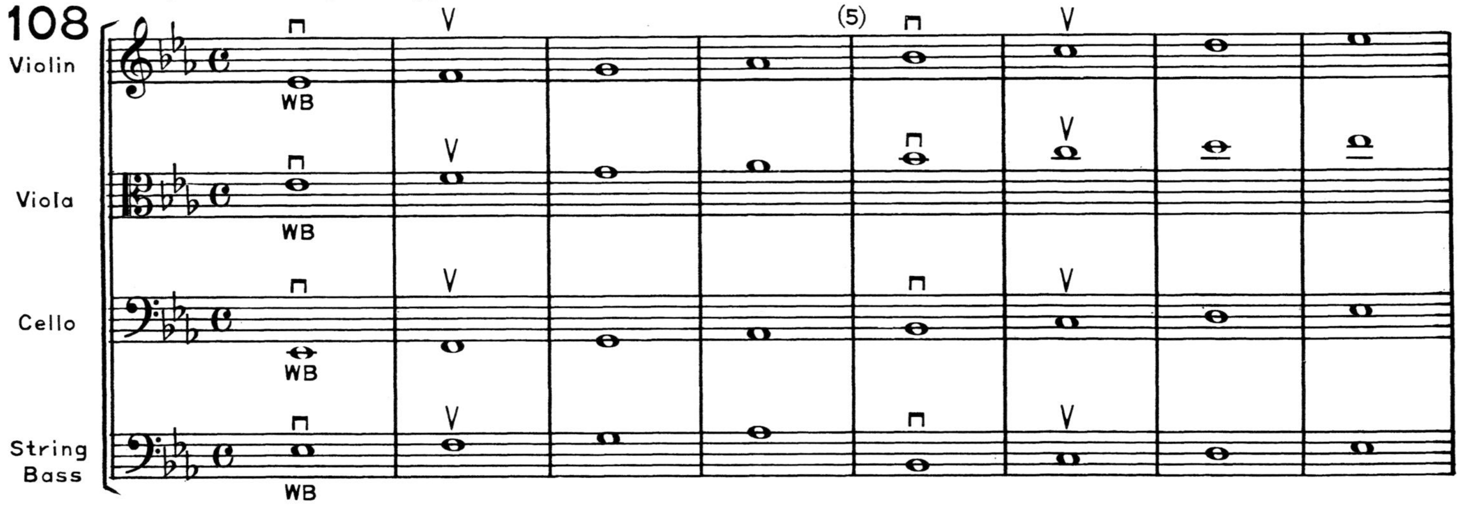

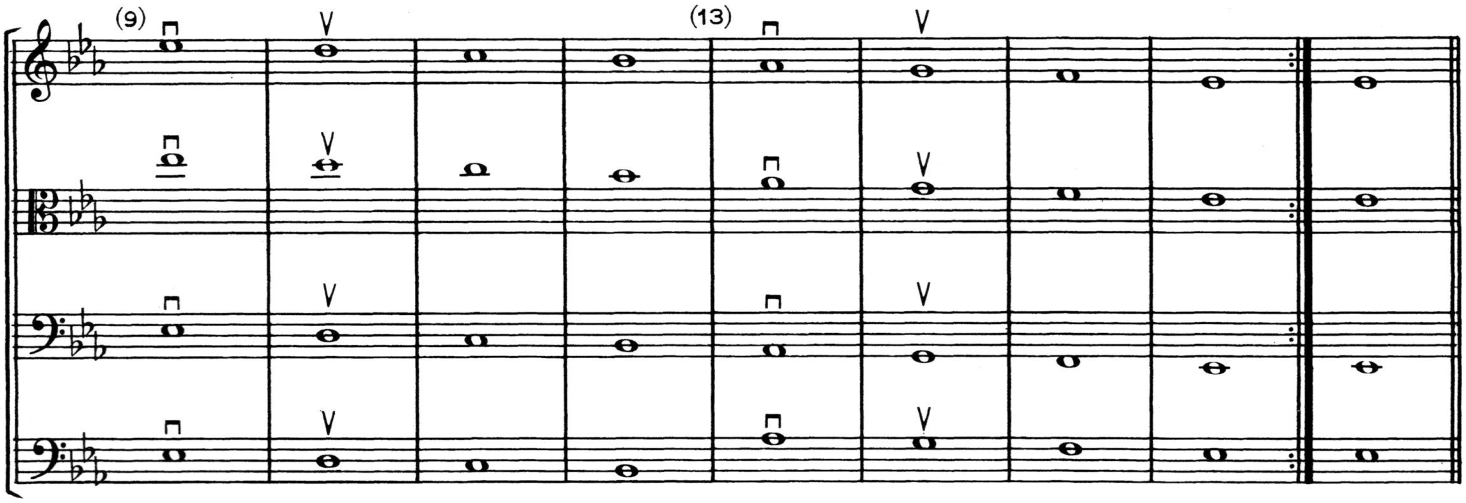

108

Eighth Notes

Also practice (1) slurring each TWO notes, and (2) slurring each FOUR notes.

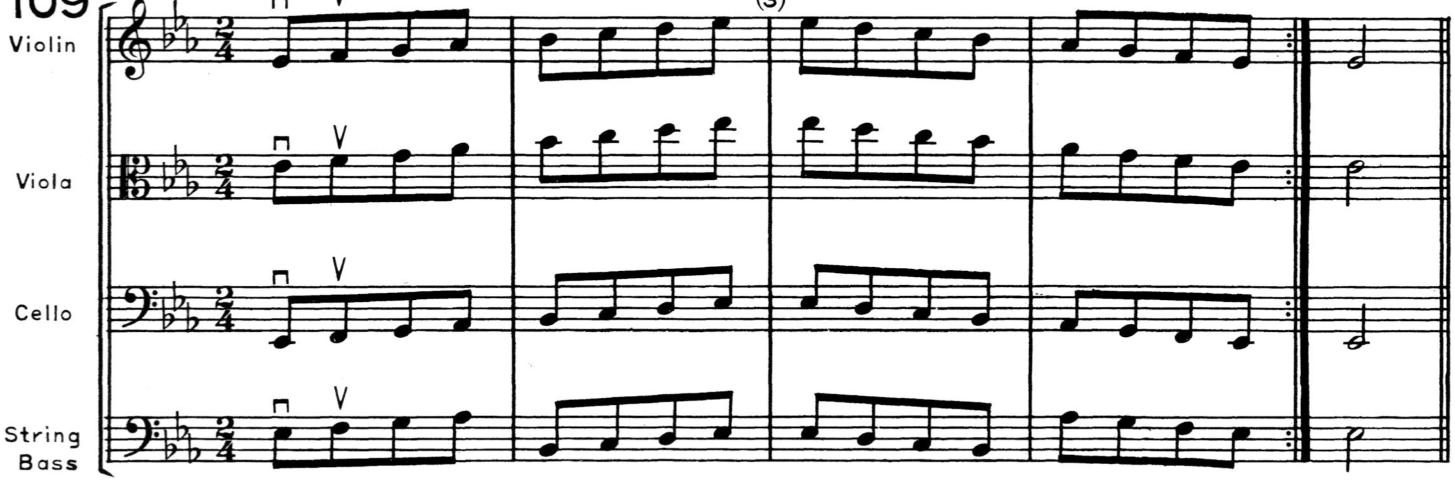

109

Quarter and Eighth Notes

Chromatic Scales

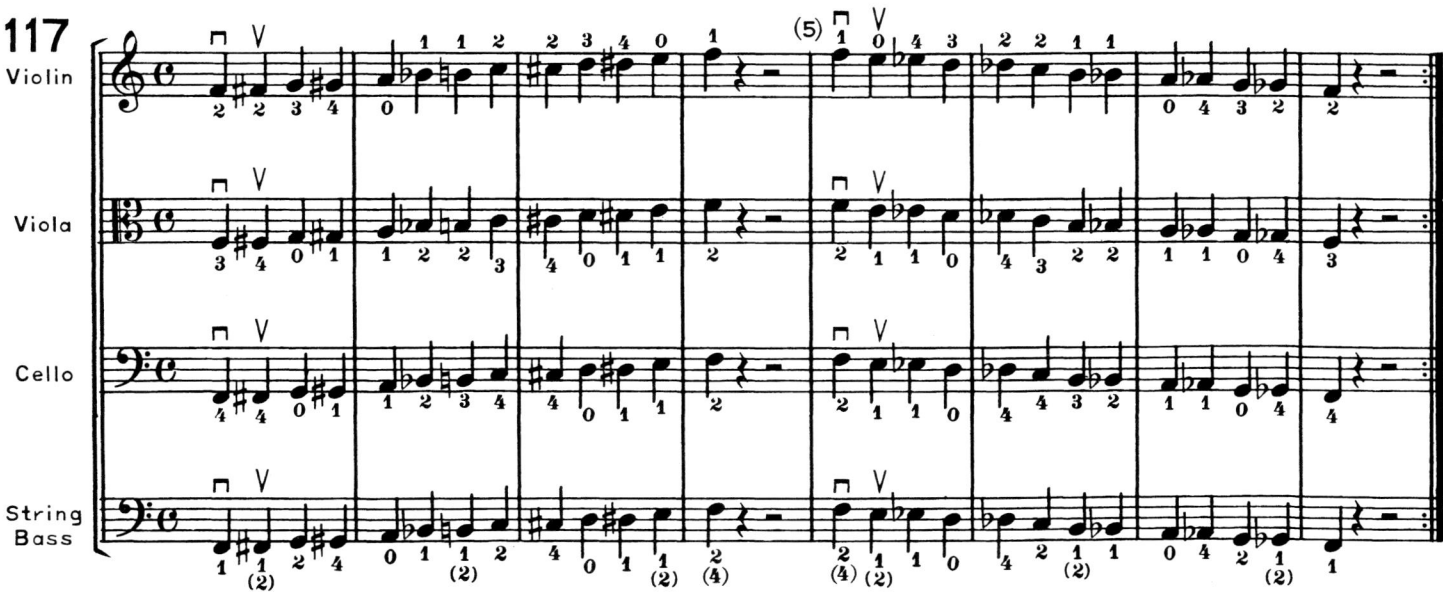
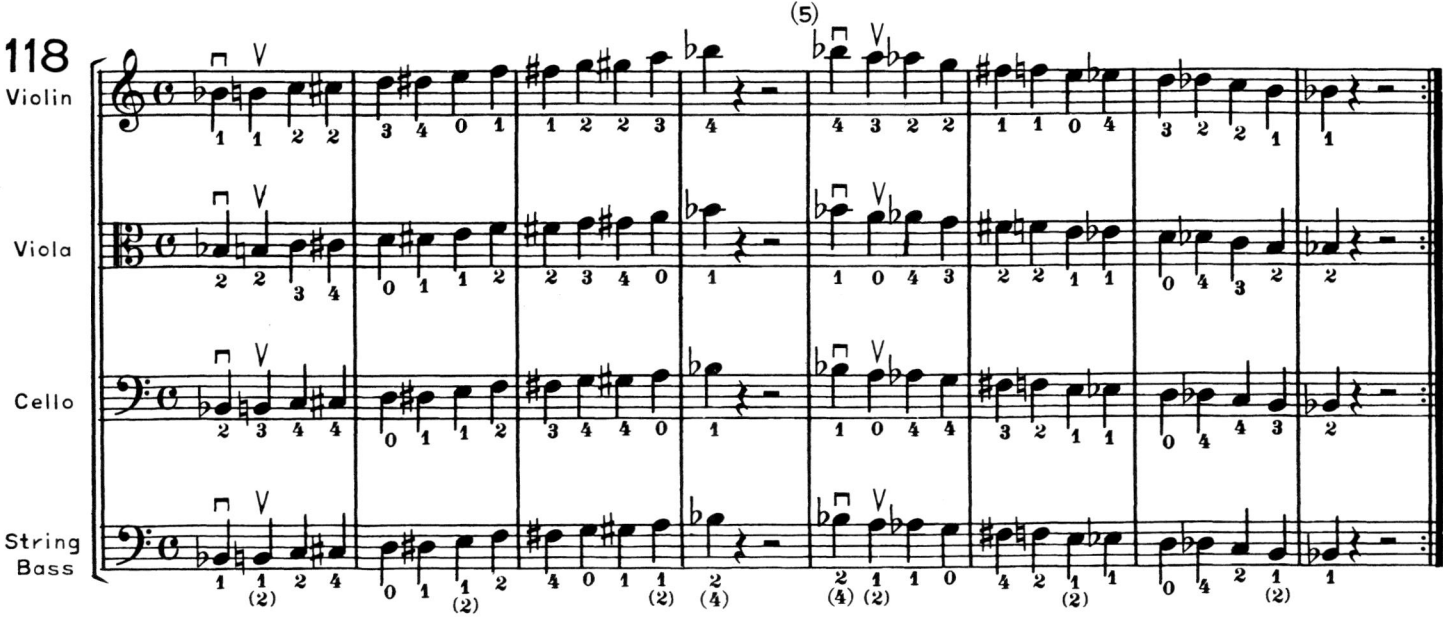

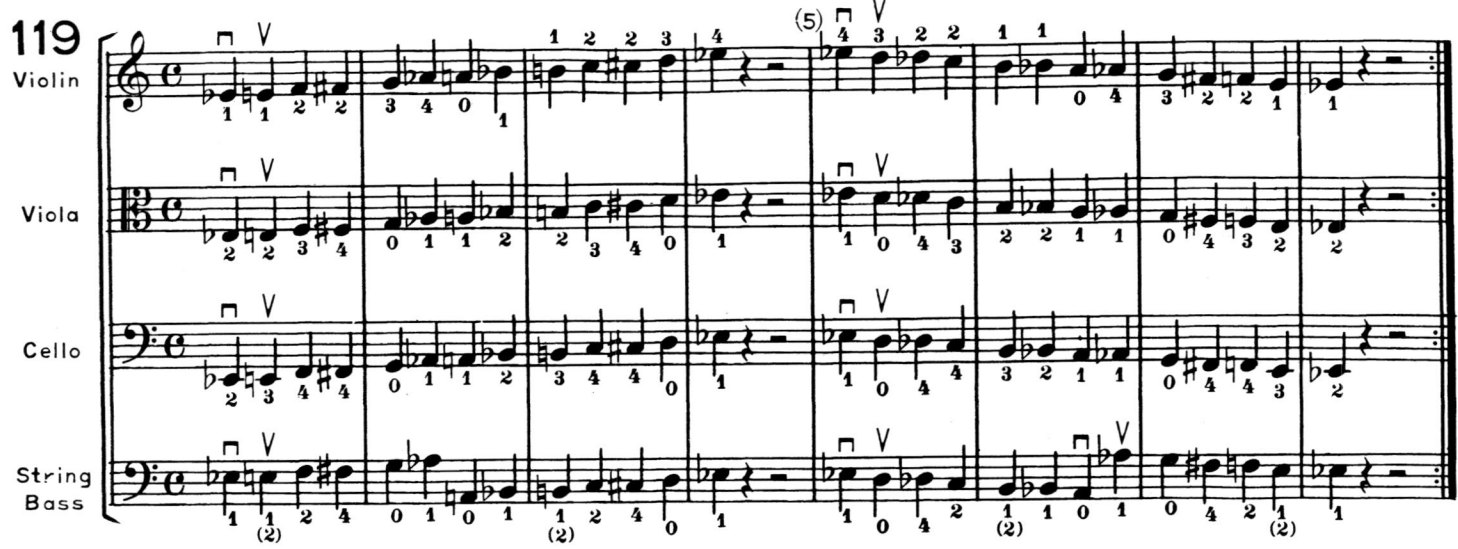

Extended Chromatic Scale

Also practice (1) slurring each TWO notes, and (2) slurring each FOUR notes on violin, viola, and cello. On string bass, where scale ascends and descends without the jumps in register, also practice (1) slurring each TWO notes, and (2) slurring each FOUR notes.

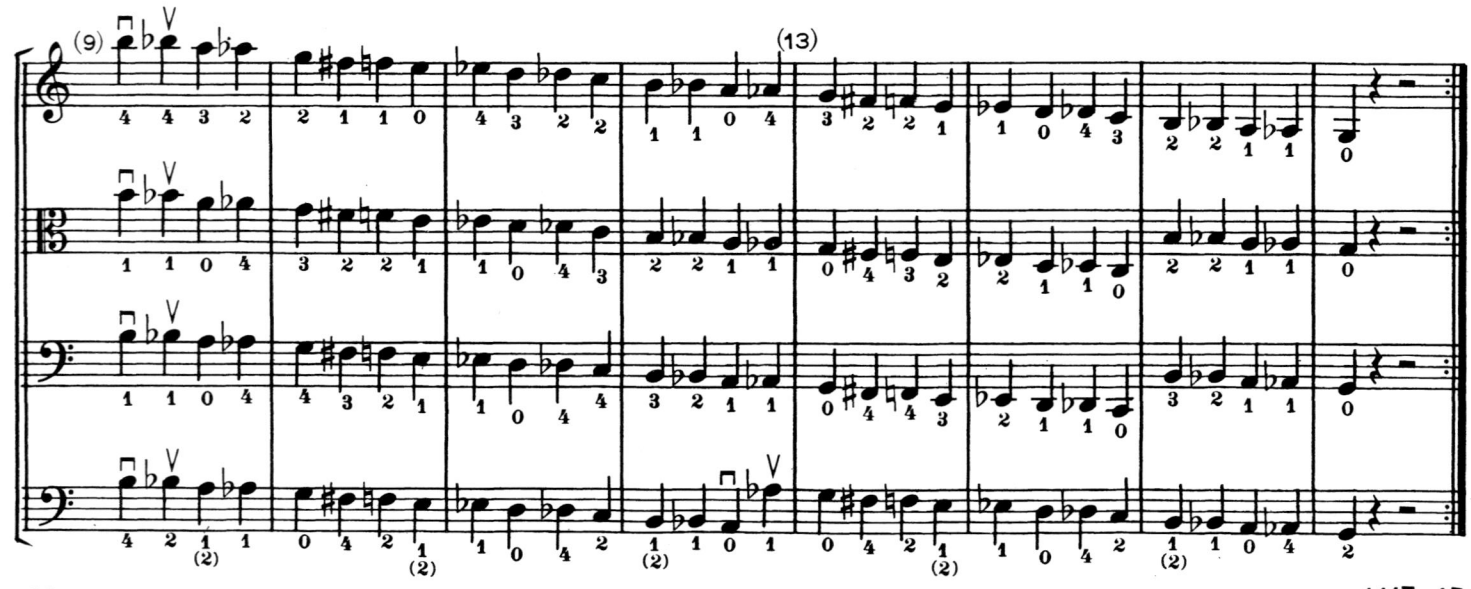